HARCOURT SCIENCE

TEACHING RESOURCES

Harcourt School Publishers

Orlando • Boston • Dallas • Chicago • San Diego

www.harcourtschool.com

Printed in the United States of America

ISBN 0-15-324481-X

7 8 9 10   082   10 09 08 07 06 05

HARCOURT SCIENCE
Contents

Harcourt

Activities for Home or School   **TR65–84**

Vocabulary Activities   **TR85–92**

Vocabulary Cards   **TR93–156**

Maps, Charts, Patterns, Graphs   **TR157–174**

School-Home Connection

Chapter Content

Our science class is beginning a chapter about cells, tissues, and body systems. We will learn that cells are the building blocks for all forms of life. Ask your child to tell you the major differences between plant and animal cells. (Plant cells have cell walls and chloroplasts.) Can these two types of cells be distinguished by sight under a microscope? (yes)

ScienceFun

Discuss with your child all the things the body does to work properly. For example, your child may think of breathing, converting food to energy, and moving blood throughout the body. As you compile your list, fill in the chart below. An example is shown.

Science Process Skills

The skill of **comparing** allows students to identify common and distinguishing characteristics among objects or events.

Talk together about a system you are both familiar with. A system could be a public transportation system, a highway system, or the heating or plumbing system of your home. Ask your child to identify the parts of the system with which he or she is familiar. Encourage your child to draw a diagram of the system, using arrows or other symbols to show how things move around the system. Then compare the system you have been discussing to a body system such as the circulatory system. Make a two-part list detailing how the systems are similar and how they are different.

What My Body Does	Parts of My Body Involved
breathing to get oxygen	nose, mouth, throat, lungs

Activity Materials from Home

Dear Family Member:

To do the activities in this chapter, we will need some materials that you may have around your home. Please note the items at the right. If possible, please send these things to school with your child.

Your help and support are appreciated!

____ **red food coloring**
____ **colored pencils**
____ **tape measure**

Harcourt

La escuela y la casa

Harcourt Ciencias

Contenido del capítulo

Nuestra clase de ciencias comienza un capítulo sobre las células, los tejidos y los sistemas del cuerpo. Aprenderemos que las células son las unidades básicas de todas las formas de vida. Pida a su hijo(a) que le diga las diferencias más importantes entre las células de las plantas y los animales. (Las células de las plantas tienen paredes celulares y cloroplastos.) ¿Se pueden distinguir estos dos tipos de células a través de un microscopio? (sí)

Diversión

Comente con su hijo(a) todas las cosas que el cuerpo hace para funcionar adecuadamente. Por ejemplo, su hijo(a) quizás piense en respirar, convertir los alimentos en energía y el movimiento de la sangre por todas las partes del cuerpo. A medida que recopila su lista, llene el cuadro de abajo. Vea el ejemplo que se muestra.

Destrezas del proceso científico

La destreza de **comparar** les permite a los estudiantes identificar características comunes y diferentes entre objetos o sucesos.

Hable con su hijo(a) sobre un sistema del cual ambos estén familiarizados. Un sistema podría ser un sistema de transporte público, un sistema de carreteras o un sistema de calefacción o tuberías de su casa. Pida a su hijo(a) que identifique las partes del sistema con el cual está familiarizado(a). Anime a su hijo para que realice un diagrama del sistema, usando flechas u otros símbolos para mostrar cómo se mueven las cosas alrededor del sistema. Luego compare el sistema que ha sido comentado por usted con un sistema del cuerpo como el sistema circulatorio. Haga una lista de dos partes detallando cómo se parecen y en qué se diferencian los sistemas.

Qué hace mi cuerpo	Partes de mi cuerpo involucradas
respirar para obtener oxígeno	nariz, boca, garganta, pulmones

Materiales de casa para la actividad

Querido familiar:

Para hacer las actividades en este capítulo, necesitaremos algunos materiales que tal vez tenga en la casa. Observe los artículos de la lista de la derecha. Si es posible, por favor envíe estas cosas con su hijo(a) a la escuela.

¡Gracias por su ayuda y su apoyo!

____ **colorante rojo**
____ **lápices de colores**
____ **cinta métrica**

Harcourt

School-Home Connection

Chapter Content

Our science class is beginning a chapter that discusses how plants, animals, and other organisms are classified.

The lessons in this chapter teach that living things are classified into five kingdoms: monerans, protists, fungi, plants, and animals. Ask your child to describe each of the different kingdoms and name organisms that belong to each of them. If your child has difficulty with this, reread parts of the chapter together, and look at the pictures.

Science Process Skills

Classifying is one of the science process skills emphasized in this chapter. Classifying involves grouping or organizing objects into categories based on specific criteria. In the chapter students classify living things into different groups and explain which features they used for their classification.

Challenge your child to come up with a classification scheme for the family's books, sports equipment, seasonal clothing, or other items. Discuss different ways to classify the items. Talk about which classification scheme would be most useful for your family and why.

Science Fun

Focusing on the classification of one living thing will help your child understand how all organisms are classified.

Ask your child to pick out one organism in which he or she has a special interest. Your child might pick out a favorite zoo animal, an exotic organism from a coral reef, or a rainforest plant. Use reference books such as encyclopedias to find the organism's scientific name. Also find the organism's species, genus, family, order, class, and phylum. Write the information in the chart.

kingdom:	
phylum:	
class:	
order:	
family:	
genus:	
species:	

Activity Materials from Home

Dear Family Member:

To do the activities in this chapter, we will need some materials that you may have around your home. Please note the items at the right. If possible, please send these things to school with your child.

Your help and support are appreciated!

____ **chenille stems**
____ **wagon-wheel pasta**
____ **candy gelatin rings**
____ **fresh celery stalks**
____ **empty juice-concentrate containers**
____ **red/blue food coloring**

Harcourt

La escuela y la casa

Contenido del capítulo

Comenzamos un capítulo en nuestra clase de ciencias que comenta cómo se clasifican las plantas, los animales y otros organismos.

Las lecciones de este capítulo enseñan que los seres vivos se clasifican en cinco reinos: móneras, protistas, hongos, plantas y animales. Pida a su hijo(a) que describa cada uno de los diferentes reinos y nombre organismos que pertenecen a cada uno de ellos. Si su hijo(a) tiene dificultad con esto, lean nuevamente las partes del capítulo y observen las ilustraciones.

Destrezas del proceso científico

Clasificar es una de las destrezas del proceso científico que se enfatizan en este capítulo. Clasificar involucra agrupar u organizar objetos en categorías basadas en un criterio específico. En el capítulo los estudiantes clasifican los seres vivos en diferentes grupos y explican qué características usaron para su clasificación.

Rete a su hijo(a) a que sugiera un esquema de clasificación para los libros de la familia, los equipos deportivos, la ropa de temporada u otros artículos. Comente diferentes maneras de clasificar los artículos. Hable sobre cuál esquema de clasificación sería más útil para su familia y por qué.

Diversión

Enfocar la clasificación de un ser vivo ayudará a su hijo(a) a comprender cómo se organizan todos los organismos.

Anime a su hijo(a) para que elija un organismo por el que tenga un interés especial. Quizás su hijo(a) elija un animal favorito del zoológico, un organismo exótico de un arrecife de coral o una planta de un bosque tropical. Use libros de referencia como enciclopedias para hallar el nombre científico del organismo. También busque la especie, el género, la familia, el orden, la clase y el fílum del organismo. Escribe la información en la tabla.

reino:	
fílum:	
clase:	
orden:	
familia:	
género:	
especie:	

Materiales de casa para la actividad

Querido familiar:

Para hacer las actividades en este capítulo, necesitaremos algunos materiales que tal vez tenga en la casa. Observe los artículos de la lista de la derecha. Si es posible, por favor envíe estas cosas con su hijo(a) a la escuela.

¡Gracias por su ayuda y su apoyo!

_____ varillas de felpilla

_____ macarrones en forma de rueda

_____ caramelos de aros de gelatina

_____ tallos de apio fresco

_____ recipientes de jugo concentrado vacíos

_____ colorante rojo, azul

Harcourt

School-Home Connection

Chapter Content

Our science class is beginning a chapter about animal growth and reproduction. The reading covers the different forms of plant and animal reproduction as well as the life cycles of living things and inherited traits. Work with your child to write down the various types of reproduction and give an example of each.

Science Fun

The following activity will prepare students for classroom investigations on animal growth and reproduction.

Look together for pictures of adult dogs or cats and their offspring. Talk about some traits of the animals in the picture. In what ways do the animals resemble one another? How are they different? Together, make a list of traits you think might be inherited. Ask your child to suggest ways that someone could test to find out whether some traits are inherited or not. For example, your child might suggest breeding several generations of puppies or kittens and keeping track of the traits each generation shows.

Science Process Skills

The skill of **using numbers** allows students to estimate and quantify data. To quantify data, students count, order, compare, use basic operations like adding, subtracting, multiplying, or dividing, and use ratios or percents.

Talk with your child about the human life cycle. Ask your child to estimate how long it lasts. If you and your child know a number of older people, you might talk about how old they are. Discuss the different stages of the human life cycle. There are many ways of talking about these stages: some may mention infancy, childhood, adolescence, young adulthood, middle age, and senior citizen as stages. Others may make fewer or more divisions. After your child suggests a list of stages, have him or her make estimates about the number of years each stage lasts. Discuss why it is hard to divide the human life cycle into stages.

Activity Materials from Home

Dear Family Member:

To do the activities in this chapter, we will need some materials that you may have around your home. Please note the items at the right. If possible, please send these things to school with your child.

Your help and support are appreciated!

____ **paper plates**
____ **mirror**

Unit A • Chapter 3

Contenido del capítulo

Nuestra clase de ciencias comienza un capítulo sobre el crecimiento y la reproducción de los animales. La lectura abarca las diferentes formas de reproducción de las plantas y los animales así como también los ciclos de vida de los seres vivos y las características hereditarias. Trabaje con su hijo(a) para escribir los varios tipos de reproducción y dé un ejemplo de cada uno.

Diversión

La siguiente actividad preparará a los estudiantes para investigaciones del salón de clases sobre el crecimiento y la reproducción de los animales.

Busque con su hijo ilustraciones de descendencias de perros adultos o gatos. Hable sobre algunas características de los animales en la ilustración. ¿De qué maneras los animales se parecen unos con otros? ¿En que se diferencian? Con su hijo(a), haga una lista de las características que usted piensa que podrían ser hereditarias. Pida a su hijo(a) que sugiera algunas formas en que alguien podría probar para hallar si algunas características son hereditarias o no. Por ejemplo, su hijo(a) podría sugerir criar varias generaciones de mascotas o gatitos y seguir la pista de las características que cada generación muestra.

Destrezas del proceso científico

La destreza de **usar números** les permite a los estudiantes estimar y cuantificar los datos. Para cuantificar datos, los estudiantes cuentan, ordenan, comparan, usan operaciones básicas como sumar, restar, multiplicar o dividir y usan la razón o los porcentajes.

Hable con su hijo(a) sobre el ciclo de vida humana. Pida a su hijo(a) que estime cuánto tiempo dura esto. Si usted y su hijo(a) conocen un número de personas mayores, debería hablar de qué tan mayores son ellos. Comente las diferentes etapas del ciclo de vida humana. Existen muchas formas de hablar sobre estas etapas: algunas podrían mencionar la infancia, la niñez, la adolescencia, la pubertad, la edad media y el ciudadano anciano como etapas. Otras quizás hagan menos o más divisiones. Después que su hijo(a) sugiera una lista de etapas, pídale que haga estimaciones sobre el número de años que cada una de las etapas dura. Comente por qué es tan difícil dividir el ciclo de vida humana en etapas.

Materiales de casa para la actividad

Querido familiar:

Para hacer las actividades en este capítulo, necesitaremos algunos materiales que tal vez tenga en la casa. Observe los artículos de la lista de la derecha. Si es posible, por favor envíe estas cosas con su hijo(a) a la escuela.

¡Gracias por su ayuda y su apoyo!

_____ **platos de papel**
_____ **espejo**

Harcourt

School-Home Connection

Chapter Content

Our science class is beginning a chapter about types of plants and their adaptations. We will be reading about the parts of plants and their functions, as well as the differences between vascular and nonvascular plants. The chapter also outlines the many different uses we have for plants. Tour your home with your child and list things made from plants. (clothing, wood furniture, some medicines, foods, and paper products such as books and paper towels)

Science Process Skills

You **compare** when you identify common and distinguishing characteristics among objects and events.

Look at plants in your environment with your child. These may be houseplants in your home or the homes of others, flower or vegetable plants in a garden, or trees or bushes in your neighborhood. Discuss what these plants have in common. How are they different? Ask your child to list three things these plants have in common and three ways they are different.

Science Fun

The following activity will prepare students for classroom investigations of plants and plant adaptations.

As you prepare a meal or a snack using plant foods, ask your child which part of the plant is being eaten. Cut open an apple, an orange, a squash, or a tomato to identify the seeds. Talk about why seeds are important to a plant. Ask your child to think about why plants have changed over time so that they enclose their seeds in these elaborate (and tasty) packages. Together, plan a meal using at least one food representing each plant part.

Plant Part Menu

celery (stalks and leaves)
carrots (roots)
spinach (leaves)
beans and rice (seeds)
whole-wheat bread (seeds)

Activity Materials from Home

Dear Family Member:

To do the activities in this chapter, we will need some materials that you may have around your home. Please note the items at the right. If possible, please send these things to school with your child.

Your help and support are appreciated!

____ **potted plant**
____ **newspaper**
____ **plastic knife**
____ **large, plastic cup**
____ **unpopped popcorn**

Harcourt

La escuela y la casa

Contenido del capítulo

Nuestra clase de ciencias comienza un capítulo sobre los tipos de plantas y sus adaptaciones. Leeremos sobre las partes de las plantas y sus funciones, así como también las diferencias entre plantas vasculares y no vasculares. El capítulo también perfila la gran cantidad de usos que tenemos para las plantas. Dé un paseo con su hijo(a) por la casa y haga una lista de las cosas hechas de las plantas. (ropas, muebles de madera, algunas medicinas, alimentos y productos de papel como libros y toallas de papel)

Destrezas del proceso científico

Usted **compara** cuando identifica características comunes y diferentes entre objetos y sucesos.

Busque con su hijo(a) plantas en su medio ambiente. Éstas podrían ser plantas caseras en su casa o en la casa de otros, flores o plantas de vegetales en un jardín o árboles o arbustos en su vecindario. Comente qué tienen estas plantas en común. ¿En qué se diferencian? Pida a su hijo(a) que haga una lista de tres cosas que estas plantas tienen en común y tres formas en que se diferencian.

Diversión

La siguiente actividad preparará a los estudiantes para investigaciones del salón de clases sobre las plantas y las adaptaciones de las plantas.

A medida que prepara una comida o un bocadillo usando plantas alimenticias, pregunte a su hijo(a) qué parte de la planta se está comiendo. Corte y abra una manzana, una naranja, una calabacita o un tomate para identificar las semillas. Hable de por qué las semillas son importantes para las plantas. Pida a su hijo(a) que piense sobre por qué las plantas han cambiado con el paso del tiempo de manera que se encierran sus semillas en estos paquetes detallados (y sabrosos). Con su hijo(a), planee una comida usando al menos un alimento que represente cada parte de una planta.

Menú de las partes de
una planta

apio (tallo y hojas)
zanahorias (raíces)
espinacas (hojas)
frijoles y arroz (semillas)
pan de trigo (semillas)

Materiales de casa para la actividad

Querido familiar:

Para hacer las actividades en este capítulo, necesitaremos algunos materiales que tal vez tenga en la casa. Observe los artículos de la lista de la derecha. Si es posible, por favor envíe estas cosas con su hijo(a) a la escuela.

¡Gracias por su ayuda y su apoyo!

____ **planta en maceta**
____ **periódico**
____ **cuchillo plástico**
____ **vaso de plástico grande**
____ **palomitas de maíz sin reventar**

Harcourt

School-Home Connection

Harcourt Science

Chapter Content

Our science class is beginning a chapter about natural cycles, including the nitrogen cycle, the carbon-oxygen cycle, and the water cycle.

ScienceFun

The following activity will prepare students for classroom investigations of natural cycles.

Discuss the idea of a cycle with your child. Your child may know the word *cycle* in the context of a wheel, as in *bicycle* or *life cycle*. Ask your child how a life cycle is like a circle. (An immature organism develops and grows to reproduce another immature organism.) Your child may also be familiar with a cycle as a route through space that brings a traveler back to his starting point without retracing the original path. Encourage your child to list three words or phrases that use the word or word part *cycle*. Then ask him or her to draw or diagram the terms to illustrate the circular aspect of cycles. Explain that some natural materials travel through a cycle of forms and uses.

Science Process Skills

The skill of **inferring** allows students to use their observations to form ideas about what might have happened.

If you have plants in or around your home talk to your child as you water them. Ask your child to think about why the plant must be watered regularly. What does the plant do with the water? Why doesn't watering plants cause Earth to run out of water? If necessary, review with your child the water cycle shown below. Encourage your child to see that although plants use water to grow, they also give off water through their leaves. Ask your child to plan a way to test this inference. If possible, help him or her follow through on this test. One way to test this idea is to place a plastic bag over a well-watered plant, and set the bag-covered plant in a sunny spot. Over time, water that has been absorbed by the roots and released by the leaves will collect on the bag as small drops.

Activity Materials from Home

Dear Family Member:

To do the activities in this chapter, we will need some materials that you may have around your home. Please note the items at the right. If possible, please send these things to school with your child.

Your help and support are appreciated!

____ **plastic straws**
____ **plastic cups**
____ **zip-top plastic bags**

Harcourt

La escuela y la casa

Harcourt Ciencias

Contenido del capítulo

Nuestra clase de ciencias comienza un capítulo sobre los ciclos naturales que se incluyen el ciclo del nitrógeno, el ciclo de carbono-oxígeno y el ciclo del agua.

Diversión

La siguiente actividad preparará a los estudiantes para las investigaciones del salón de clases de los ciclos naturales.

Comente con su hijo(a) la idea de un *ciclo*. Quizás su hijo(a) conoce la palabra ciclo en el contexto de una rueda como en una *bicicleta* o en el *ciclo de vida*. Pregunte a su hijo(a) cómo el ciclo de vida es como un círculo. (Un organismo inmaduro se desarrolla y crece para reproducir otro organismo inmaduro.) Su hijo(a) también puede estar familiarizado con un ciclo como una ruta a través del espacio que regresa a un viajero a su punto de partida sin trazar de nuevo su ruta original. Anime a su hijo(a) a enumerar tres palabras o frases que usan la palabra o parte de la palabra *ciclo*. Luego pídale que haga un dibujo o un diagrama de los términos para ilustrar el aspecto circular de lo ciclos. Explique que algunos materiales naturales viajan a través de un ciclo de formas y usos.

Destrezas del proceso científico

La destreza de **inferir** les permite a los estudiantes que usen sus observaciones para formar ideas sobre lo que hubiera podido suceder.

Si tiene plantas en o alrededor de su casa, hable con su hijo(a) mientras las riega. Pida a su hijo(a) que piense en por qué la planta se debe regar regularmente. ¿Qué hace la planta con el agua? ¿Por qué la Tierra no se queda sin agua si regamos las plantas? Si es necesario, repase con su hijo(a) el ciclo del agua que se muestra abajo. Anime a su hijo(a) a ver que aunque las plantas usan agua para crecer, ellas también emiten agua a través de sus hojas. Pida a su hijo(a) que planee una manera de probar esta inferencia. Si es posible, ayúdelo a seguir con su prueba. Una manera de probar esta idea es colocar una bolsa de plástico sobre una planta que esté bien regada y colocarla donde le dé el Sol. Con el tiempo, el agua que las raíces han absorbido y han emitido las hojas, se acumularán en la bolsa en forma de gotitas.

Materiales de casa para la actividad

Querido familiar:

Para hacer las actividades en este capítulo, necesitaremos algunos materiales que tal vez tenga en la casa. Observe los artículos de la lista de la derecha. Si es posible, por favor envíe estas cosas con su hijo(a) a la escuela.

¡Gracias por su ayuda y su apoyo!

____ **pajitas de plástico**
____ **vasos de plástico**
____ **bolsas de plástico con cierre**

Harcourt

School-Home Connection

Harcourt Science

Chapter Content

Our science class is beginning a chapter about the ways that living things interact. We will learn about ecosystems, food chains, and food webs. We will also study the survival adaptations of certain plants and animals. The chapter concludes with a discussion about extinction and vanishing habitats. With your child, research an endangered plant or animal. Why is it endangered? Brainstorm a list of some solutions to the endangered species' plight.

Science Fun

The following activity will prepare students for classroom investigations of the interactions of living things.

With your child, examine your kitchen, your home, and your environment at large and make a list of all the plant and animal products you notice. (Be sure to include plant products like cotton, rubber, cardboard, and paper.) Then ask your child to classify them as plant or animal products. Discuss the many ways we depend on other organisms for food and objects we use.

Science Process Skills

The skill of **predicting** allows students to use their observations to form ideas about what might happen in the future.

If you happen to live near the site of a major natural disaster like a forest fire, volcanic activity, or a severe hurricane, discuss with your child how the natural landscape regenerated itself after the disaster.

If you do not live near such a site, ask your child what he or she thinks happens to a forest that has been burned. Discuss how plants and animals return in stages: first small plants and the animals that depend on them for food and habitat, and then, as larger plants have time to grow back, larger animals. Reinforce this concept by reading together the book *The Mountain That Loved a Bird* by Alice McLerran.

Activity Materials from Home

Dear Family Member:

To do the activities in this chapter, we will need some materials that you may have around your home. Please note the items at the right. If possible, please send these things to school with your child.

Your help and support are appreciated!

____ **garden gloves**
____ **garden trowel**
____ **aluminum pan**
____ **paper towels**
____ **toothpicks**
____ **yarn**
____ **large green cloth**

Harcourt

La escuela y la casa

Harcourt Ciencias

Contenido del capítulo

Hoy comenzamos un capítulo de ciencias sobre las maneras en que se relacionan los seres vivos. Aprenderemos de los ecosistemas, las cadenas alimenticias y las redes alimenticias. También estudiaremos las adaptaciones de supervivencia de algunas plantas y animales. El capítulo concluye con una conversación sobre la extinción y desaparición de hábitats. Con su hijo(a), investigue una planta o un animal en peligro. ¿Por qué está en peligro? Haga una tormenta de ideas para hacer una lista de algunas soluciones del compromiso de la especie en peligro.

Diversión

La siguiente actividad preparará a los estudiantes para las investigaciones del salón de clases de las relaciones de los seres vivos.

Con su hijo(a), examine su cocina, su casa y su ambiente, y haga una lista de todos los productos de plantas y animales que encuentren. (Asegúrese de incluir productos de plantas como algodón, goma, cartulina y papel.) Luego pida a su hijo(a) que los clasifique como productos de plantas o animales. Comente las diferentes maneras en que dependemos de otros organismos para la comida y los objetos que usamos.

Destrezas del proceso científico

La destreza de **predecir** les permite a los estudiantes usar sus observaciones para formar ideas sobre lo que podría suceder en el futuro.

Si llegara a vivir cerca de un lugar de un desastre natural importante como un incendio forestal, actividad volcánica o un huracán riguroso, comente con su hijo(a) cómo el paisaje natural se regeneró por sí mismo después del desastre.

Si no vive cerca de tal lugar, pregunte a su hijo(a) lo que cree que le sucede a un bosque que se ha incendiado. Comente cómo las plantas y los animales regresan en etapas: primero las plantas pequeñas y los animales que dependen de ellas para comer y como hábitat y después, a medida que crecen plantas más grandes, animales más grandes. Refuerce este concepto leyendo el libro *The Mountain That Loved a Bird* de Alice McLerran.

Materiales de casa para la actividad

Querido familiar:

Para hacer las actividades en este capítulo, necesitaremos algunos materiales que tal vez tenga en la casa. Observe los artículos de la lista de la derecha. Si es posible, por favor envíe estas cosas con su hijo(a) a la escuela.

¡Gracias por su ayuda y su apoyo!

____ guantes para el jardín
____ pala de jardín
____ bandeja de aluminio
____ toallas de papel
____ palillos de dientes
____ estambre
____ tela verde grande

Harcourt

School-Home Connection

Chapter Content

Our science class is beginning a chapter about land biomes and water ecosystems. Activities in this chapter include comparing and drawing conclusions about the relationships between biomes and climate zones. We will also be observing organisms in a pond community to infer whether they are producers or consumers.

Science Process Skills

The skill of **comparing** requires students to make observations about the similarities and differences between two or more objects or events.

If you can, visit two or more natural ecosystems with your child. These could be nearby locations like a local pond, riverbank, meadow, forest, or marsh. If you are unable to do this, recall previous visits to such places. Ask your child to think about ways the two ecosystems were similar and different from one another. Encourage your child to compare the ecosystems in a table, or to make collages or a mobile that points out the major aspects of each ecosystem.

Science Fun

The following activity will prepare students for classroom investigations of land biomes and climate zones.

Use a world map or globe to play a game. Each player says "my name is . . ." and states a name that begins with a letter of the alphabet. As an example, the first player says, "My name is Abigail" and the second player says, "My name is Bob." (The progression continues in alphabetical order.) Then each player names a country, continent, city, or region that begins with the same letter and says something they will take to that place that begins with that letter as well. This game will have the added twist of requiring that the object the character takes be suitable for the climate of the place the player names. Thus, the first player might say, "My name is Abigail. I'm going to the Arctic, and I'm taking an anorak." The second player could say, "My name is Bob. I'm going to Borneo, and I'm taking rain boots." Keep playing as time allows or until you have played through the alphabet.

Ecosystem	Similar	Different

Harcourt

La escuela y la casa

Harcourt Ciencias

Contenido del capítulo

Nuestra clase de ciencias comienza un capítulo sobre los biomas terrestres y los ecosistemas acuáticos. Las actividades en este capítulo incluyen comparar y sacar conclusiones sobre las relaciones entre los biomas y las zonas climáticas. También observaremos organismos en una comunidad de un estanque para inferir si son productores o consumidores.

Destrezas del proceso científico

La destreza de **comparar** requiere que los estudiantes hagan observaciones sobre las semejanzas y las diferencias entre dos o más objetos o eventos.

Si puede, visite con su hijo(a) dos o más ecosistemas naturales. Éstos pueden ser lugares cercanos como un estanque local, las orillas de un río, una pradera, un bosque o un pantano. Si no puede hacer esto, recuerde visitas anteriores a lugares como éstos. Pida a su hijo(a) que piense en las maneras en que los dos ecosistemas se parecían y se diferenciaban el uno del otro. Anime a su hijo(a) a comparar los ecosistemas en una tabla o a hacer collages o un móvil que señale los aspectos más importantes de cada ecosistema.

Diversión

La siguiente actividad preparará a los estudiantes para las investigaciones del salón de clases de los biomas terrestres y las zonas climáticas.

Usa un mapamundi para jugar un juego. Cada jugador dice — mi nombre es…— y expresa un nombre que comience con una letra del alfabeto. Por ejemplo, el primer jugador dice: —Mi nombre es Abigail— y el segundo jugador dice: —Mi nombre es Bob—. (La secuencia continúa en orden alfabético). Luego cada jugador nombra un país, un continente, una ciudad o una región que comience con la misma letra y dice algo que llevaría a ese lugar que también comience con esa letra. A este juego se le dará un giro adicional al pedirle al jugador que el objeto que nombre se ajuste al clima del lugar. Entonces, el primer jugador podría decir: —Mi nombre es Abigail. Voy al Ártico y llevo un abrigo—. El segundo jugador podría decir: —Mi nombre es Bob. Voy a Borneo y llevo botas—. Sigan jugando hasta que el tiempo lo permita o hasta que hayan jugado diciendo todo el alfabeto.

Ecosistema	Semejanza	Diferencia

Harcourt

School-Home Connection

Chapter Content

Our science class is beginning a chapter about threats to ecosystems and things that humans can do to protect and preserve ecosystems.

Science Fun

The following activity will prepare students for classroom investigations of threats to ecosystems and how to protect them.

Read with your child books such as *50 Simple Things You Can Do to Save the Earth* and *50 Simple Things Kids Can Do to Save the Earth* by The Earth Works Group. Which of these suggestions is being practiced in your community? Which could be put into practice? Are there any drawbacks to some of the suggestions? Together, list reasons why some of the suggestions are not implemented. Then invite your child to offer suggestions of additional behaviors that could be adopted or encouraged in your community. Identify the pros and cons of each suggestion. Record your ideas in the table below.

Science Process Skills

The skill of **using models** allows students to use their observations to form ideas about what might have happened.

In a park, a forest, or a backyard, have your child discuss the variety of organisms that rely on a tree or pond for food and habitat. Then ask your child to discuss the organisms that can rely on a parking lot or housing development for habitat. Discuss the different impacts of these two ways of using land. Brainstorm with your child creative ways to reduce the harm to existing ecosystems when development occurs. Here are some ideas you could discuss.

- Including green space and trees around all buildings and parking lots

- Making sure water running off parking lots is not directed toward ponds or lakes

- Encouraging people to leave undisturbed any animals and plants that are growing in the green areas

Environmental Idea	Pros	Cons

Activity Materials from Home

Dear Family Member:

To do the activities in this chapter, we will need some materials that you may have around your home. Please note the items at the right. If possible, please send these things to school with your child.

Your help and support are appreciated!

____ plastic dishpan
____ potting soil
____ liquid fertilizer
____ shoe box
____ plastic wrap
____ gravel
____ sand

Harcourt

La escuela y la casa

Contenido del capítulo

Nuestra clase de ciencias comienza un capítulo sobre las amenazas a los ecosistemas y las cosas que los seres humanos pueden hacer para proteger y conservar los ecosistemas.

Diversión

La siguiente actividad preparará a los estudiantes para las investigaciones del salón de clases de las amenazas a los ecosistemas y cómo protegerlos.

Lea con su hijo(a) libros como *50 Simple Things You Can Do to Save the Earth* and *50 Simple Things Kids Can Do to Save the Earth* por The Earth Works Group. ¿Cuál de estas sugerencias se practica en su comunidad? ¿Cuál se podría poner en práctica? ¿Hay alguna desventaja para algunas de las sugerencias? Enumeren razones de por qué no se pueden implementar algunas de las sugerencias. Luego invite a su hijo(a) a ofrecer sugerencias de comportamientos adicionales que se podrían adoptar o estimular en su comunidad. Identifique los pro y los contra de cada sugerencia. Anote sus ideas en la siguiente tabla.

Destrezas del proceso científico

La destreza de **usar modelos** les permite a los estudiantes usar sus observaciones para formar ideas sobre lo que hubiera podido suceder.

En un parque, un bosque o un patio, pida a su hijo(a) que comente la variedad de organismos que dependen de un árbol o un estanque para comer y vivir. Luego pida a su hijo(a) que comente los organismos que pueden depender de un estacionamiento o un desarrollo habitacional como hábitat. Comente el impacto diferente de estas dos maneras de usar la tierra. Con su hijo(a) haga una tormenta de ideas sobre las maneras creativas de reducir el daño de los ecosistemas existentes cuando ocurre el desarrollo. Aquí hay algunas ideas que podrían comentar.

- Incluir áreas verdes y árboles alrededor de todos los edificios y estacionamientos

- Asegurarse de que el agua que escurre de los estacionamientos no se dirige hacia las lagunas o los lagos

- Animar a las personas a no molestar a cualquier animal o planta que crece en las áreas verdes

Idea ambiental	Pros	Contra

Materiales de casa para la actividad

Querido familiar:

Para hacer las actividades de este capítulo, necesitaremos algunos materiales que tal vez tenga en la casa. Observe los artículos de la lista de la derecha. Si es posible, por favor envíe estas cosas con su hijo(a) a la escuela.

¡Gracias por su ayuda y su apoyo!

____ **fregadero de plástico**
____ **tierra para plantar**
____ **fertilizante líquido**
____ **basura**
____ **caja de zapatos**
____ **papel de plástico**
____ **gravilla**
____ **arena**

Harcourt

School-Home Connection

Chapter Content

Our science class is beginning a chapter about changes to Earth's surface. We will be learning about slow changes to the surface, such as weathering and erosion, and dramatic changes by forces, like earthquakes and volcanoes. Students will also study the forces that cause continents to move.

Science**Fun**

The following activity will prepare students for classroom investigations of Earth's surface.

With your child, page through books or magazines with photographs of different landscapes. A book with photographs of National Parks or magazines such as *National Geographic* would have these kinds of photographs. Discuss the landforms and features shown in the photographs. For example, ask your child to comment on different types of mountains, plateaus, river valleys, or other features shown. Invite your child to speculate about how such landscapes might have formed. Use the table to help keep track of your ideas.

Science Process Skills

Observing involves using one or more of the senses to perceive properties of objects and events. People use their senses of sight, hearing, smell, taste, and touch to observe the world around them. Observing is the most basic science skill, and it is the foundation for other skills of science like inferring, comparing, classifying, and measuring.

As you travel through your community with your child, whether on foot, by bus, or in a car, help your child strengthen his or her powers of observation by playing simple games. For example, ask how many yellow things he or she sees, how many rectangular shapes, how many things with wheels, or how many living things. To further reinforce observation skills as well as memory, ask your child when you return home to relate through drawings or a story the observations made during the trip.

Landform	How Formed

Activity Materials from Home

Dear Family Member:

To do the activities in this chapter, we will need some materials that you may have around your home. Please note the items at the right. If possible, please send these things to school with your child.

Your help and support are appreciated!

____ **small plastic bags**
____ **graham crackers**
____ **plastic spoons**

La escuela y la casa

Harcourt Ciencias

Contenido del capítulo

Nuestra clase de ciencias comienza un capítulo sobre los cambios de la superficie de la Tierra. Aprenderemos sobre los cambios lentos en la superficie como la degradación y la erosión y los cambios drásticos por las fuerzas como los terremotos y los volcanes. Los estudiantes estudiarán también las fuerzas que causan el movimiento de los continentes.

Diversión

La siguiente actividad preparará a los estudiantes para investigaciones del salón de clases sobre la superficie de la Tierra.

Con su hijo(a), dé un vistazo a los libros o revistas con ilustraciones de diferentes formaciones terrestres. Un libro con ilustraciones de parques nacionales o revistas como *National Geographic* podría tener estos tipos de ilustraciones. Comente con su hijo(a) las formaciones terrestres y las características que se muestran en las ilustraciones. Por ejemplo, pida a su hijo(a) que comente los diferentes tipos de montañas, mesetas, valles de ríos u otras características mostradas. Pida a su hijo(a) que especule sobre cuántas formaciones terrestres se podrían haber formado. Use la tabla para anotar sus ideas.

Destrezas del proceso científico

Observar significa usar uno o más de los sentidos para percibir las propiedades de los objetos y de los sucesos. Las personas usan sus sentidos de la visibilidad, el auditivo, del olfato, del gusto y del tacto para observar el mundo que los rodea. Observar es la destreza más fundamental de las ciencias y es la base para otras destrezas de la ciencia como inferir, comparar, clasificar y medir.

A medida que da un paseo con su hijo(a) por la comunidad, ya sea a pie, en autobús o en un carro, ayude a su hijo(a) a fortalecer sus poderes de observación jugando juegos sencillos. Por ejemplo, pregunte cuántas cosas amarillas, cuántas formas rectangulares, cuántas cosas con ruedas o cuántos seres vivientes puede ver. Para reforzar adicionalmente las destrezas de observación como la memoria, cuando regresen a su casa pida a su hijo(a) que relacione las observaciones realizadas durante el paseo en una ilustración o en una historia.

Formación terrestre	Cómo se formó

Materiales de casa para la actividad

Querido familiar:

Para hacer las actividades en este capítulo, necesitaremos algunos materiales que tal vez tenga en la casa. Observe los artículos de la lista de la derecha. Si es posible, por favor envíe estas cosas con su hijo(a) a la escuela.

¡Gracias por su ayuda y su apoyo!

____ bolsas plásticas pequeñas
____ galletas de harina de trigo
____ cucharas de plástico

Harcourt

School-Home Connection

Harcourt Science

Chapter Content

Our science class is beginning a chapter about rocks and minerals. We will be learning about how scientists define minerals and how minerals are related to rocks. We will also be learning about the three main ways that rocks form.

Science Process Skills

Classifying is one of the science process skills emphasized in this chapter. Classifying involves grouping objects that have similar properties. Once categories have been established, classifying also involves deciding which group a particular object belongs in. This simple activity will help your child practice identifying rocks.

Look through the chapter in your child's science book. Use your hand or a piece of paper to cover up the picture captions. Challenge your child to identify the rocks pictured as igneous, sedimentary, or metamorphic. Have your child identify the characteristics of the rock that helped him or her classify it.

Science Fun

You can help your child remember how sedimentary rocks are formed, and have a tasty treat in the process!

What You Need
- 2 slices of bread
- sandwich fixings, such as lunch meat, cheese, lettuce, tomato
- mustard or mayonnaise

What to Do

1. Put one slice of bread on a plate.
2. Spread mustard or mayonnaise on the bread.
3. Make a distinct layer of each fixing.
4. Top with the second piece of bread.
5. Cut the sandwich in half. As you each eat, talk about how the sandwich is like sedimentary rock layers. (Many sedimentary rocks are formed as sediments are deposited in layers. The oldest layer is on the bottom, and was deposited first. The youngest layer is on top, and was deposited last.)

Activity Materials from Home

Dear Family Member:

To do the activities in this chapter, we will need some materials that you may have around your home. Please note the items listed at the right. If possible, please send these things to school.

Your help and support are appreciated!

____ **plain, white tiles**
____ **pennies**
____ **steel nails**
____ **white vinegar**
____ **paper towels**
____ **aluminum pie pan**
____ **aquarium gravel**

La escuela y la casa

Contenido del capítulo

Nuestra clase de ciencias comienza un capítulo sobre las rocas y los minerales. Aprenderemos cómo los científicos definen los minerales y cómo los minerales están relacionados con las rocas. También aprenderemos las tres maneras principales de la formación de las rocas.

Destrezas del proceso científico

Clasificar es una de las destrezas del proceso científico enfatizado en este capítulo. Clasificar significa agrupar objetos que tienen propiedades similares. Una vez que las categorías han sido establecidas, clasificar significa también decidir a cuál grupo pertenece un objeto en particular. Esta actividad simple ayudará a su hijo(a) a practicar la identificación de las rocas.

Repase el capítulo en el libro de ciencias de su hijo(a). Use su mano o un pedazo de papel para cubrir el título de la ilustración. Rete a su hijo(a) para que identifique las rocas ilustradas como la ígnea, la sedimentaria o la metamórfica. Pida a su hijo(a) que identifique las características de la roca que lo ayudan a clasificarla.

Diversión

¡Usted puede ayudar a su hijo(a) a recordar cómo se forman las rocas sedimentarias y saborear algo sabroso en el proceso!

Lo que necesitas

- 2 rebanadas de pan
- ingredientes para preparar un sándwich como carne, queso, lechuga, tomate
- mostaza o mayonesa

Lo que vas a hacer

1. Coloquen una rebanada de pan en un plato.
2. Unten mostaza o mayonesa en el pan.
3. Coloquen una capa distinta de cada uno de los ingredientes con que va a preparar el sándwich.
4. Pongan la segunda rebanada de pan.
5. Corten el sándwich por la mitad. Mientras cada uno va comiendo, comenten en qué se parece el sándwich a las capas de rocas sedimentarias. (Muchas de las rocas sedimentarias se forman a medida que los sedimentos se van depositando en capas. La capa más vieja está en la parte de abajo y se depositó primero. La capa más nueva está en la parte de arriba y se depositó de último.)

Materiales de casa para la actividad

Querido familiar:

Para hacer las actividades en este capítulo, necesitaremos algunos materiales que tal vez tenga en la casa. Observe los artículos de la lista de la derecha. Si es posible, por favor envíe estas cosas con su hijo(a) a la escuela.

¡Gracias por su ayuda y su apoyo!

_____ **azulejos blancos sencillos**
_____ **monedas de 1 ¢**
_____ **clavos de acero**
_____ **vinagre blanco**
_____ **toallas de papel**
_____ **bandeja de aluminio para pastel**
_____ **gravilla para acuario**

Harcourt

School-Home Connection

Harcourt Science

Chapter Content

Our science class is beginning a chapter about weather and climate. The readings cover measuring of weather conditions, wind and its effects on the weather, and the different climates that exist on Earth.

Science Fun

Talk with your child about any weather events that are in the news or have been in the news recently. Look for newspaper or news magazine stories about hurricanes, droughts, floods, record snowfalls, or other major weather events. Read the articles together and look at any photographs. Discuss why these stories are important. How are these weather conditions affecting people in these areas? Recall with your child any local weather events. Then ask him or her to write a news story to report the event.

What was the event?

Where did the event happen?

When did the event happen?

Who was affected?

How were they affected?

Science Process Skills

You **measure** weather conditions when you use a tool like a thermometer, rain gauge, or barometer to collect data. Measuring is sometimes regarded as a form of comparing—to measure, you compare a unit on a tool (like inches or degrees) to the object you are measuring (like rainfall or temperature).

Discuss different aspects of the weather. Temperature, wind speed and direction, humidity, and precipitation all affect the weather. Ask your child how each of these aspects is measured. Discuss some reasons for measuring them. (to keep records, make predictions, provide an objective standard rather than individual perceptions) Choose an aspect of weather to measure and set up a "measuring station." Then with your child, watch television news weather reports over the course of one week. Compare the measurements the two of you gathered with those given by the television meteorologist. How do they compare? Discuss possible reasons for any discrepancies.

Activity Materials from Home

Dear Family Member:

To do the activities in this chapter, we will need some materials that you may have around your home. Please note the items at the right. If possible, please send these things to school with your child.

Your help and support are appreciated!

- ____ **clean, empty cans with lids removed**
- ____ **garden trowel**
- ____ **dry potting soil**

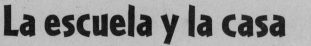

La escuela y la casa

Harcourt Ciencias

Contenido del capítulo

Nuestra clase de ciencias comienza un capítulo sobre el tiempo y el clima. Las lecturas cubren la medida de las condiciones del tiempo, el viento y sus efectos sobre el clima y los diferentes climas que existen en la Tierra.

Diversión

Hable con su hijo(a) sobre cualquier suceso del tiempo que esté en las noticias o que haya estado recientemente. Observe los periódicos o las historias en las noticias de las revistas sobre huracanes, sequías, inundaciones, registros de nevadas u otro suceso climatológico importante. Con su hijo(a) lea los artículos y observe cualquier ilustración. Comente por qué son importantes estas historias. ¿Cómo estas condiciones del tiempo afectan a las personas en estas áreas? Con su hijo(a) recuerde cualquier suceso climatológico local. Luego pídale que escriba una historia de noticias para reportar el suceso.

¿**Cuál** fue el suceso?

¿**Dónde** sucedió el suceso?

¿**Cuándo** sucedió el suceso?

¿**Quién** fue afectado?

¿**Cómo** los afectó?

Destrezas del proceso científico

Cuando usted usa una herramienta como un termómetro, un pluviómetro o un barómetro para recopilar datos, usted **mide** las condiciones del tiempo. Medir es considerado a veces como una forma de comparar, para medir, usted compara una unidad en una herramienta (como en pulgadas o en grados) con el objecto que usted está midiendo (como la precipitación o la temperatura).

Comente con su hijo(a) los diferentes aspectos del clima. La temperatura, la velocidad y la dirección del viento, la humedad y la precipitación afectan el clima. Pregunte a su hijo(a) cómo son medidos cada uno de estos aspectos. Comente algunas razones por las que son medidos. (para mantener registros, hacer predicciones, proporcionar un objetivo específico en vez de percepciones individuales) Elija un aspecto del clima para medir y establezca una "estación de medida". Luego con su hijo(a), observe las noticias del reporte del tiempo en la televisión durante el transcurso de una semana. Con su hijo(a) compare las medidas que recopilaron con las que dio el meteorólogo de la televisión. ¿En qué se parecen? Comente con su hijo(a) las razones posibles de cualquier discrepancia.

Materiales de casa para la actividad

Querido familiar:

Para hacer las actividades de este capítulo, necesitaremos algunos materiales que tal vez tenga de la casa. Observe los artículos de la lista de la derecha. Si es posible, por favor envíe estas cosas con su hijo(a) a la escuela.

¡Gracias por su ayuda y apoyo!

_____ latas vacías sin tapas, limpias
_____ pala de jardín
_____ tierra seca para plantar

Harcourt

School-Home Connection

Chapter Content

Our science class is beginning a chapter about ocean exploration. We will study the movement of water in the ocean, interactions between land and ocean, and resources within the ocean.

Science Fun

With your child, look at a globe in your home or the library. Talk about how much of Earth is covered by oceans. Compare the size of the oceans with the size of the United States or North America. Review with your child anything he or she already knows about the ocean such as waves, saltiness, and ocean life. Explain that scientists still have a great deal to learn about the oceans. Ask your child why it has been so difficult for humans to explore the oceans. (Your child might suggest difficulties in breathing under water or the dangers of water pressure.)

Science Process Skills

You **observe** things when you use your senses to note the properties of an object, such as a shoreline. Help your child practice the skill of observation by taking a walk with her or him along the shoreline of any body of water— ocean, river, lake, or pond—near you.

Ask your child to note ways that the shoreline is different from land back away from the shore. Be sure to include observations of senses other than sight. For example, is there a difference in smell between the two areas? What about the incidence of plant and animal life? If this is a river, it might be the difference between the shore and the land five feet away from the river. If it is the ocean, it may be the difference between the beach or shore and the land a quarter of a mile away. Record your observations in the table below.

Observations

Land	Water	Where Land and Water Meet

Activity Materials from Home

Dear Family Member:

To do the activities in this chapter, we will need some materials that you may have around your home. Please note the items at the right. If possible, please send these things to school with your child.

Your help and support are appreciated!

___ **drinking straws**
___ **shoe boxes**
___ **sand**
___ **pebbles or small rocks**

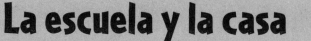

La escuela y la casa

Harcourt Ciencias

Contenido del capítulo

Nuestra clase de ciencias comienza un capítulo sobre la exploración del océano. Estudiaremos el movimiento del agua en el océano. Las relaciones entre la tierra y el océano y los recursos dentro del océano.

Diversión

Con su hijo(a), observe un globo terráqueo en su casa o en la librería. Hable sobre cuánto de la Tierra está cubierta por los océanos. Compare el tamaño de los océanos con el tamaño de Estados Unidos o Norte América. Repase con su hijo(a) cualquier cosa que ya sabe sobre los océanos como las olas, la salobridad y la vida del océano. Explíquele que los científicos todavía tienen mucho que aprender sobre los océanos. Pregunte a su hijo(a) por qué ha sido tan difícil para los humanos explorar los océanos. (Su hijo(a) quizás sugiera dificultades para respirar debajo del agua o los peligros de la presión del agua.)

Destrezas del proceso científico

Usted **observa** cosas cuando usa sus sentidos para observar las propiedades de algo como la orilla de la playa. Ayude a su hijo(a) para que practique la destreza de observación realizando una caminata a lo largo de la orilla de cualquier masa de agua, océano, río, lago o estanque, cerca de usted.

Pida a su hijo(a) que observe las formas en que se diferencian las orillas de la tierra que se encuentra detrás de la parte de afuera de la orilla. Asegúrese de incluir observaciones con otros sentidos y no sólo con el de la vista. Por ejemplo, ¿existe alguna diferencia de olor entre las dos áreas? ¿Qué hay de la incidencia en la vida de una planta o un animal? Si es un río, la diferencia puede estar entre la orilla y la tierra que se encuentra a cinco pies de distancia del río. Si es un océano, la diferencia puede estar entre la playa u orilla y la tierra a un cuarto de milla de distancia. Anote sus observaciones en la tabla de abajo.

Observaciones

Tierra	Agua	¿Dónde se unen la tierra y el agua?

Materiales de casa para la actividad

Querido familiar:

Para hacer las actividades de este capítulo, necesitaremos algunos materiales que tal vez tenga en la casa. Observe los artículos de la lista de la derecha. Si es posible, por favor envíe estas cosas con su hijo(a) a la escuela.

¡Gracias por su ayuda y apoyo!

_____ **pajitas de beber**
_____ **cajas de zapatos**
_____ **arena**
_____ **canicas o rocas pequeñas**

Harcourt

School-Home Connection

Harcourt Science

Chapter Content

Our science class is beginning a chapter about Earth and its moon and their relationship to the sun. We will be learning about moon phases as well as eclipses of the moon and the sun.

ScienceFun

The following activity will prepare students for classroom investigations of Earth and the moon.

Use the newspaper, a calendar, or an almanac to find out when the next full moon will occur. If the night of the full moon or the nights just before or after the full moon are clear, go outside to look at the moon with your child. Share any stories or information you may have about the influence of the moon on crops, people, the tides, and so forth. Invite your child to think about why human beings have been so curious about the moon. Ask your child to recall stories, legends, or nursery rhymes she or he may know about the moon. If desired, continue observing over time the other phases of the moon. Challenge your child to draw pictures of each phase and the position of Earth and the sun when that phase is visible.

Science Process Skills

Inferring involves the use of logical reasoning to make conclusions based on observations. Inferences are explanations of events. Inferences are based on judgments and are not always correct. Inferences supported by observations and reasoning are always valid, however, whether or not they are correct.

Discuss things your child may know about the moon. For example, your child probably knows that astronauts who walked on the moon needed to wear protective space suits. Look at a picture of such an astronaut in your child's textbook or another book. Ask your child to make an inference about conditions on the moon based on logical reasoning and observations of the space suit.

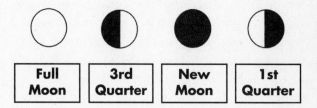

| Full Moon | 3rd Quarter | New Moon | 1st Quarter |

Activity Materials from Home

Dear Family Member:

To do the activities in this chapter, we will need some materials that you may have around your home. Please note the items at the right. If possible, please send these things to school with your child.

Your help and support are appreciated!

____ beach ball
____ baseball
____ Ping-Pong ball
____ newspapers
____ aluminum pans
____ flour
____ marbles

Harcourt

La escuela y la casa

Contenido del capítulo

Nuestra clase de ciencias comienza un capítulo sobre la Tierra y la Luna y su relación con el Sol. Aprenderemos sobre las fases de la Luna así como los eclipses de la Luna y del Sol.

Diversión

La siguiente actividad preparará a los estudiantes para las investigaciones del salón de clases sobre la Tierra y la Luna.

Use un periódico, un calendario o un almanaque para determinar cuándo habrá la siguiente Luna llena. Si la noche de Luna Llena o las noches justo antes de la Luna Llena están despejadas, salga con su hijo(a) y observe la Luna. Comparta cualquier historia o información que quizás usted tenga sobre la influencia de la Luna en las cosechas, las personas, las mareas y así sucesivamente. Pida a su hijo(a) que piense en por qué los seres humanos han estado tan fascinados por la Luna. Anímelo a recordar historias, leyendas o, versos infantiles que sepan sobre la Luna. Si lo desea, continúe observando las otras fases de la Luna por un tiempo. Rete a su hijo(a) para que haga ilustraciones de cada fase y la posición de la Tierra y el Sol cuando se vea la fase.

Destrezas del proceso científico

Inferir significa el uso de un razonamiento lógico para sacar conclusiones basadas en observaciones. Las inferencias son explicaciones de sucesos y están basadas en juicios y no siempre son correctas. Las inferencias basadas en observaciones y razonamientos son siempre válidas, ya sea, si son o no correctas.

Comente cosas que quizás su hijo(a) sepa sobre la Luna. Por ejemplo, tal vez su hijo(a) sepa si los astronautas que caminaron en la Luna tuvieron que usar trajes protectores espaciales. Observe una ilustración de un astronauta en el libro de texto de su hijo(a) o en otro libro. Pídale que haga una inferencia sobre las condiciones de la Luna basada en un razonamiento lógico y en observaciones del traje espacial.

Luna Llena	Tercer Menguante	Luna Nueva	Primer Menguante

Materiales de casa para la actividad

Querido familiar:

Para hacer las actividades en este capítulo, necesitaremos algunos materiales que tal vez tenga en la casa. Observe los artículos de la lista de la derecha. Si es posible, por favor envíe estas cosas con su hijo(a) a la escuela.

¡Gracias por su ayuda y su apoyo!

_____ **pelota de playa**
_____ **pelota de béisbol**
_____ **pelota de tenis de mesa**
_____ **periódicos**
_____ **bandejas de aluminio**
_____ **harina**
_____ **canicas**

Harcourt

School-Home Connection

Chapter Content

Our science class is beginning a chapter about the sun and other stars. We will be learning about the sun's energy, star brightness, and galaxies.

ScienceFun

On a clear night, go outside with your child to see how many stars you can see in the sky. Even in a place with many lights, the brightest stars can be seen on a clear night. Use the space below to make a simple map locating the brightest stars you see. Look for any visible variations in color. If you can, use a book about backyard astronomy to find out the names of the brightest stars you see (but see activity under **Science Process Skills** before you identify the brightest stars).

Science Process Skills

A **hypothesis** is an educated guess about the relationships between variables. A hypothesis must be testable (and can be shown to be wrong). A hypothesis is based upon observation, prior knowledge, and prior experimental outcomes. A hypothesis is often altered, based on the outcomes of experiments used to test it.

Give your child a chance to practice hypothesizing by asking him or her to guess which of the bright stars in the sky are planets. Have him or her review what he or she knows about planets and stars. (Planets are closer; they orbit the sun. Stars are farther away; they don't orbit the sun.) Explain to your child that his or her hypothesis can be tested by observing the possible planets for several nights over the course of a week or ten days. The bodies that change position (as they orbit the sun) are planets.

The Night Sky

Activity Materials from Home

Dear Family Member:

To do the activities in this chapter, we will need some materials that you may have around your home. Please note the items at the right. If possible, please send these things to school with your child.

Your help and support are appreciated!

____ **large pieces of cardboard**
____ **40-watt light bulbs**
____ **60-watt light bulbs**

Harcourt

La escuela y la casa

Harcourt Ciencias

Contenido del capítulo

Nuestra clase de ciencias comienza un capítulo sobre el Sol y otras estrellas. Aprenderemos sobre la energía solar, el brillo de las estrellas y las galaxias.

Diversión

En una noche despejada, salga con su hijo(a) para ver cuántas estrellas pueden ubicar en el cielo. Incluso en un lugar con muchas luces, se pueden ver las estrellas brillantes en una noche despejada. Use el espacio siguiente para hacer un mapa sencillo ubicando las estrellas brillantes que ve. Busque cualquier variación visible de colores. Si puede, use un libro sobre el campo de astronomía para buscar los nombres de las estrellas brillantes que ve (pero vea la actividad de **Destrezas del proceso científico** antes de identificar las estrellas brillantes).

Destrezas del proceso científico

Una **hipótesis** es una estimación razonada sobre las relaciones entre las variables. Una hipótesis se debe verificar (y puede comprobarse que está equivocada). Una hipótesis está basada en una observación, un conocimiento previo y en resultados de experimentos previos. Una hipótesis a menudo se altera debido a resultados de los experimentos usados para comprobarla.

Dé a su hijo(a) la oportunidad para que practique la formulación de hipótesis preguntando cuál de las estrellas que brillan en el cielo son planetas. Anímelo a repasar lo que sabe sobre los planetas y las estrellas. (Los planetas están más cerca; ellos giran en órbita alrededor del Sol. Las estrellas están alejadas de ellos; ellas orbitan el Sol.) Explique a su hijo(a) que su hipótesis puede comprobarse observando la cantidad de planetas posible durante varias noches por el transcurso de una semana o de diez días. Los cuerpos que cambian de posición (como los que orbitan el Sol) son planetas.

El cielo nocturno

Materiales de casa para la actividad

Querido familiar:

Para hacer las actividades en este capítulo, necesitaremos algunos materiales que tal vez tenga en la casa. Observe los artículos de la lista de la derecha. Si es posible, por favor envíe estas cosas con su hijo(a) a la escuela.

¡Gracias por su ayuda y su apoyo!

_____ pedazos grandes de cartulina
_____ bombillos de 40 vatios
_____ bombillo de 60 vatios

Harcourt

School-Home Connection

Chapter Content

Our science class is beginning a chapter about matter and its properties. The readings cover physical properties and how to measure some of them. They tell how physical properties can be used to identify substances. The chapter then describes the three common states of matter and talks about how substances change state. It discusses physical and chemical changes, and tells how physical changes can be used to identify substances and to separate mixtures. Finally, the law of conservation of matter is described.

Science **Fun**

The following activity will prepare students for classroom investigations about matter and its properties.

Take your child to the library and find a handbook of chemistry. Look up the physical properties of specific substances, such as iron and oxygen. See how many different facts you can find out about water. You will find water listed in several places in the index.

Science Process Skills

When students **observe,** they are using their senses to learn about something. When students **infer,** they use logical reasoning to make conclusions based on observations. Observations are facts. Inferences are explanations for events that are based on judgments. Any inference that uses observation and logical reasoning is valid, but it may not be correct.

Give your child the chance to practice observing and making inferences. One of the physical properties he or she will be studying is density. You can describe the density of a material by comparing it to the density of water. Anything that floats in water is less dense than water. Drop a penny into a glass of water. Is the penny's density more or less than that of water? Try a marshmallow. It floats, so it is less dense than water. Try an ice cube. Is solid water (ice) more or less dense than liquid water? Because it floats, it must be less dense. Now chip a small piece off of the ice cube and try it in the water. It behaves the same as the entire ice cube. No matter how much of a substance you have, its density stays the same.

Activity Materials from Home

Dear Family Member:

To do the activities in this chapter, we will need some materials that you may have around your home. Please note the items at the right. If possible, please send these things to school with your child.

Your help and support are appreciated!

____ **apples**
____ **zip-top bags**
____ **baking soda**
____ **cornstarch**
____ **talcum powder**
____ **baking powder**
____ **vinegar**

La escuela y la casa

Harcourt Ciencias

Contenido del capítulo

Nuestra clase de ciencias comienza un capítulo sobre la materia y sus propiedades. Las lecturas cubren las propiedades físicas y cómo medir algunas de ellas. Dicen cómo las propiedades físicas se pueden usar para identificar las substancias. Después, el capítulo describe los tres estados comunes de la materia y habla de cómo cambian de estado las substancias. Éste habla sobre cómo los cambios físicos se pueden usar para identificar las substancias y para separar las mezclas. Finalmente se describe la ley de la conservación de la materia.

Diversión

La siguiente actividad preparará a los estudiantes para las investigaciones del salón de clases sobre la materia y sus propiedades.

Lleve a su hijo(a) a la biblioteca y busque un manual de química. Busquen las propiedades físicas de substancias específicas como el hierro y el oxígeno. Vean cuántos factores diferentes pueden hallar sobre el agua. Ustedes hallarán el agua enumerada en lugares diferentes del índice.

Destrezas del proceso científico

Cuando los estudiantes **observan**, usan sus sentidos para aprender sobre algo. Cuando los estudiantes **infieren**, usan el razonamiento lógico para hacer conclusiones basadas en sus observaciones. Las observaciones son hechos. Las inferencias son explicaciones para los eventos basados en juicios. Cualquier inferencia que usa la observación y el razonamiento lógico es válida pero quizás no es correcta.

Dé a su hijo(a) la oportunidad de practicar la observación y hacer inferencias. Una de las propiedades físicas que estará estudiando es la densidad. Usted puede describir la densidad de un material comparándolo con la densidad del agua. Cualquier cosa que flota en el agua es menos denso que el agua. Deje caer una moneda de 1¢ en un vaso de agua. ¿Es la densidad de la moneda de 1¢ mayor o menor que la del agua? Pruebe con un malvavisco. Éste flota, así que es menos denso que el agua. Pruebe con un cubo de hielo. ¿Tiene el agua sólida (hielo) mayor o menor densidad que el agua líquida? Debido a que flota, debería ser menos denso. Ahora quítale un pedacito al cubo de hielo y pruébalo en el agua. Éste se comporta igual que todo el cubo de hielo. No importa qué cantidad de una substancia tengas, su densidad permanece igual.

Materiales de casa para la actividad

Querido familiar:

Para hacer las actividades en este capítulo, necesitaremos algunos materiales que tal vez tenga en la casa. Observe los artículos de la lista de la derecha. Si es posible, por favor envíe estas cosas con su hijo(a) a la escuela.

¡Gracias por su ayuda y su apoyo!

_____ **manzanas**
_____ **bolsas con cierre**
_____ **bicarbonato**
_____ **maicena**
_____ **talco en polvo**
_____ **polvo de hornear**
_____ **vinagre**

Harcourt

School-Home Connection

Chapter Content

Our science class is beginning a chapter about atoms and elements. The readings cover the structure of atoms. Common elements, their properties, and the Periodic Table are also discussed. Confirm your child's understanding of the structure of matter by asking him or her to define or explain the vocabulary terms in Lesson 1. Read through and review sections of the lesson, if necessary.

Science Fun

Look at the illustrations in a book such as *Powers of Ten* by Philip and Phylis Morrison, *The Secret Family* by David Bodanis, or another book that offers a view of the world at the atomic level. Talk about the shapes and arrangements these illustrations reveal. What other things do they look like? Encourage your child to choose an atomic structure and make a model or drawing based on that shape. Display the model or drawing so your child can explain the structure to other family members.

Science Process Skills

When students **infer,** they use logical reasoning to make conclusions based on observations. Inferences are explanations for events that are based on judgments. Any inference that uses observation and logical reasoning is valid, but it may not be correct.

Give your child the chance to practice making inferences by asking him or her to make observations about an event. For example, if you come in after doing an errand, ask your child what he or she observes about you and see if an inference can be made about where you have been or what you have done. To further reinforce this reasoning, make this activity a game and play it when the opportunity arises.

Activity Materials from Home

Dear Family Member:

To do the activities in this chapter, we will need some materials that you may have around your home. Please note the items at the right. If possible, please send these things to school with your child.

Your help and support are appreciated!

____ **small boxes that can be sealed**
____ **foil**
____ **balloons**

La escuela y la casa

Harcourt Ciencias

Contenido del capítulo

Nuestra clase de ciencias comienza un capítulo sobre los átomos y los elementos. Las lecturas cubren la estructura de los átomos. También se comentan los elementos comunes, sus propiedades y la Tabla periódica. Confirme la comprensión de su hijo(a) sobre la estructura de la materia pidiéndole, si es necesario, que defina o explique los términos de vocabulario de la lección.

Diversión

Observe las ilustraciones en un libro como *Powers of Ten* de Philip y Phylis Morrison, *The Secret Family* de David Bodanis, u otro libro que ofrezca una vista del mundo al nivel atómico. Hable sobre las formas y los arreglos que revelan estas ilustraciones. ¿A qué otras cosas se parecen? Anime a su hijo(a) a elegir una estructura atómica y hacer un modelo o dibujo basado en esa forma. Exhiba el modelo o dibujo para que su hijo(a) pueda explicar la estructura a otros familiares.

Destrezas del proceso científico

Cuando los estudiantes **infieren**, usan el razonamiento lógico para hacer conclusiones basadas en observaciones. Las inferencias son explicaciones para los eventos basados en juicios. Cualquier inferencia que usa la observación y el razonamiento lógico es válida pero quizás no es correcta.

Dé a su hijo(a) la oportunidad de practicar cómo hacer inferencias pidiéndole que haga observaciones sobre un evento. Por ejemplo, si usted llega después de hacer una diligencia, pídale a su hijo(a) que lo observe para ver si puede hacer una inferencia acerca de dónde ha estado usted o lo que ha hecho. Para reforzar más este razonamiento, haga de esta actividad un juego y háganlo cuando llegue la oportunidad.

Materiales de casa para la actividad

Querido familiar:

Para hacer las actividades en este capítulo, necesitaremos algunos materiales que tal vez tenga en la casa. Observe los artículos de la lista de la derecha. Si es posible, por favor envíe estas cosas con su hijo(a) a la escuela.

¡Gracias por su ayuda y su apoyo!

_____ cajas pequeñas que se puedan sellar
_____ chapa
_____ globos

Harcourt

School-Home Connection

Harcourt Science

Chapter Content

Our science class is beginning a chapter about physical forces such as gravitation and magnetism and how they affect objects on Earth. The chapter covers forces such as friction, gravity, and magnetism. It also explains the concept of work and the help that simple machines can provide in doing work.

Look for simple and compound machines around your home. Have your child attempt to classify the type of simple machine represented or to identify the simple machines within any compound machines.

Science**Fun**

The following activity will prepare students for classroom investigations of physical forces.

Discuss rides your child may have taken at amusement parks or carnivals. How did force, speed, motion, and direction affect those rides to make them fun or scary? Guide your child in imaging an amusement ride that they would like to ride. Suggest that he or she draw a model of the ride in the space. Would physical forces allow this ride to really exist?

Science Process Skills

The skill of **interpreting data** involves many other process skills, such as making predictions, inferences, and hypotheses from a set of data. Interpretations may need revisions after additional data has been obtained.

Ask your child to experiment with dropping different things outside. Objects your child might experiment with include small pieces of tissue, buttons, pieces of hardware, and a tennis ball or other "bouncy" object. Ask your child to observe the way each item falls and then make an inference to explain these differences. Then encourage your child to plan an investigation that would attempt to make the falling results more even. Is such a thing possible?

Object	How It Falls

My Amusement Ride

Harcourt

La escuela y la casa

Harcourt Ciencias

Contenido del capítulo

Nuestra clase de ciencias comienza un capítulo sobre las fuerzas físicas como la gravitación y el magnetismo y su efecto sobre los objetos de la Tierra. El capítulo estudia las fuerzas tales como la fricción, la gravedad y el magnetismo. También explica el concepto de trabajo y cómo algunas máquinas simples pueden ayudar en el trabajo.

Busque en su casa algunas máquinas simples y compuestas. Pida a su hijo(a) que trate de clasificar el tipo de máquina simple representada o que identifique las máquinas simples que se encuentran dentro de las máquinas compuestas.

Diversión

La actividad siguiente preparará a los estudiantes para las investigaciones del salón de clase sobre las fuerzas físicas.

Comente sobre los aparatos que su hijo(a) ha disfrutado en los parques de diversión o en las ferias. ¿Cómo la fuerza, la velocidad, el movimiento y la dirección afectan esos aparatos para que sean divertidos o den miedo? Guíe a su hijo(a) para que se imagine qué aparato le gustaría experimentar. Sugiérale que dibuje un modelo del aparato. ¿Creen realmente que las fuerzas físicas permitirían que existiera este aparato?

Destrezas del proceso científico

La destreza para **interpretar datos** está relacionada con las destrezas de otros procesos, tales como hacer predicciones, inferencias y formular hipótesis a partir de un conjunto de datos. Quizás sea necesario revisar las interpretaciones después de obtener más datos.

Anime a su hijo(a) para que trate de lanzar objetos hacia afuera. Los objetos que su hijo(a) pudiera utilizar incluyen trozos de papel, botones, herramientas y una pelota de tenis u otro objeto que "rebote". Pida a su hijo(a) que observe la forma en que cada objeto cae y que luego, haga una inferencia que explique estas diferencias. Después, anime a su hijo(a) para que planifique una investigación que trate de igualar los resultados de la caída. ¿Es esto posible?

Objeto	Cómo cae

Mi aparato de diversión

Harcourt

School-Home Connection

Chapter Content

Our science class is beginning a chapter about the science of motion. Students will read about the relationship between speed and motion, the laws of motion, and the orbits of the planets. Review the laws of motion with your child by having him or her state for you these laws. If necessary, read through Lesson 2 as a means of clarifying any misunderstandings. Then guide your child in coming up with simple investigations to test the principle of each law of motion.

Science Fun

The following activity will prepare students for classroom investigations of motion.

Throw a basketball or rubber ball back and forth with your child. As you throw the ball, discuss the factors that put it in motion, cause it to stop, and influence how quickly it moves and in what direction. Experiment with bouncing the ball in different ways. Ask your child to attempt to predict the outcomes of the different bounces.

Science Process Skills

The skill of **hypothesizing** about experiments can advance thinking and increase understanding.

Discuss automobile safety features such as seat belts and air bags. Ask your child to form a hypothesis about what happens to people in a car that crashes into something and comes to a sudden stop. (The car stops, but the people keep moving forward at the speed the car was traveling.)

Discuss how seat belts and air bags help in that situation. (They stop the forward motion of the person in the car.) Ask your child to hypothesize why it is important to wear a seat belt even in a car that is equipped with an air bag. (The seat belt can keep a person from moving into the air bag as it inflates. Also, many air bags only inflate when a car is hit from the front. Many car crashes involve being hit from the rear or from the side.) Explain to your child the function of crash dummies used by car manufacturers in safety tests.

Activity Materials from Home

Dear Family Member:

To do the activities in this chapter, we will need some materials that you may have around your home. Please note the items at the right. If possible, please send these things to school with your child.

Your help and support are appreciated!

____ **clear plastic bottle/cap**
____ **board**
____ **wood blocks**
____ **dime**
____ **quarter**
____ **string**
____ **metal washers**

Harcourt

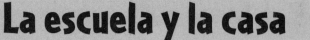

La escuela y la casa

Contenido del capítulo

Nuestra clase de ciencias comienza un capítulo sobre la ciencia del movimiento. Los estudiantes leerán sobre la relación entre la velocidad y el movimiento, sobre las leyes del movimiento y sobre las órbitas de los planetas.

Repase con su hijo(a) las leyes del movimiento pidiéndole que se las repita. Si es necesario, lea bien la lección 2 para aclarar cualquier malentendido. Luego, guíe a su hijo(a) a través de una simple investigación para que pruebe el principio de cada una de las leyes del movimiento.

Diversión

La actividad siguiente preparará a los estudiantes para las investigaciones del salón de clases sobre el movimiento.

Juegue a la pelota con su hijo(a) utilizando una pelota de básquetbol o una de goma. Mientras lanza la pelota, comente los factores que hacen que ésta se ponga en movimiento, se detenga, desarrolle cierta velocidad y tome una dirección. Haga rebotar la pelota de formas diferentes. Pida a su hijo(a) que trate de predecir los resultados de los rebotes diferentes.

Destrezas del proceso científico

La destreza de **formular hipótesis** en experimentos, puede desarrollar el razonamiento y aumentar la comprensión.

Comente las características de seguridad en los automóviles, como los cinturones de seguridad y las bolsas de aire. Pida a su hijo(a) que formule una hipótesis sobre lo que le sucedería a las personas que van en un carro que choca con algo y se detiene de repente. (El carro se para, pero las personas se mueven hacia adelante a la velocidad a la que se desplazaba el carro).

Comente en qué forma los cinturones de seguridad y las bolsas de aire ayudan en tal situación. (Detienen el movimiento hacia adelante de la persona que va en el carro). Pida a su hijo(a) que formule una hipótesis sobre la importancia de usar el cinturón de seguridad, incluso en un carro equipado con bolsa de aire. (El cinturón de seguridad evita que la persona se deslice hacia la bolsa de aire mientras ésta se infla). Además, muchas bolsas de aire se inflan sólo cuando el carro es golpeado por el frente. (En muchos accidentes, los carros son golpeados por detrás o por un lado). Explique a su hijo(a) por qué las fábricas de automóviles utilizan muñecos en las pruebas de seguridad.

Materiales de casa para la actividad

Querido familiar:

Para hacer las actividades de este capítulo, necesitaremos algunos materiales que tal vez tenga en la casa. Observe los artículos de la lista de la derecha. Si es posible, por favor envíe estas cosas con su hijo(a) a la escuela.

¡Gracias por su ayuda y su apoyo!

____ **botella de plástico transparente con tapa**
____ **pizarrón**
____ **bloques de madera**
____ **moneda de 10¢**
____ **moneda de 25¢**
____ **hilo**
____ **arandelas de metal**

Harcourt

School-Home Connection

Harcourt Science

Chapter Content

Our science class is beginning a chapter about forms of energy. Ask your child to name the many forms of energy covered in this chapter. To be certain that your child understands the differences among them, ask him or her to give examples of each. You might also encourage diagramming to show the effects of the energy forms.

Science Fun

The following activity will prepare students for classroom investigations of forms of energy.

Your child has probably experienced a power failure at some time in his or her life. Discuss with your child what it was like to temporarily lose electric power due to weather or technical problems. What things stopped working? What things continued to work? What kind of failure would have to occur to get the things that still worked to stop working? Discuss other forms of energy that were available during the power failure. Perhaps you had candles or a battery-powered flashlight, not to mention the energy from the sun itself.

Science Process Skills

The skill of **predicting** requires students to anticipate outcomes of future events, based on patterns of experience.

Use a rubber ball to discuss potential and kinetic energy. Ask whether or not the ball has energy when sitting on the floor. Then roll the ball, and ask, where did the energy come from? (Your body provided the energy to set the ball in motion.)

Set the ball on the edge of a table or counter-top. Again ask whether the ball has energy. (It has potential energy.) Let the ball fall off the edge and bounce. (The ball shows kinetic energy when it is in motion.)

Discuss the idea of potential energy, the energy an object has because of where it is or of its condition. Put the ball in different places and talk about whether its potential energy increases or decreases in each situation. (The higher the ball is, the more potential energy it has.) Ask your child to predict where the ball could be placed for maximum potential energy.

Activity Materials from Home

Dear Family Member:

To do the activities in this chapter, we will need some materials that you may have around your home. Please note the items at the right. If possible, please send these things to school with your child.

Your help and support are appreciated!

____ **tennis ball**
____ **corrugated cardboard, 12 in. by 12 in.**
____ **small mirror**
____ **metal butter knife**
____ **foam cups**
____ **plastic knife**

La escuela y la casa

Harcourt Ciencias

Contenido del capítulo

Nuestra clase de ciencias comienza un capítulo sobre las formas de energía. Pida a su hijo(a) que nombre las formas de energía estudiadas en este capítulo. Para estar seguro de que él/ella comprende las diferencias entre ellas, pídale que le dé ejemplos de cada una. Usted quizás también lo anime para que haga un diagrama y muestre los efectos de las formas de energía.

Diversión

La siguiente actividad preparará a los estudiantes para las investigaciones del salón de clases sobre las formas de energía.

Su hijo(a) probablemente ha experimentado alguna vez una falla eléctrica en su vida. Comente cómo es la pérdida temporal de la electricidad debido al clima o a problemas técnicos. ¿Qué cosas dejan de funcionar? ¿Qué cosas continúan funcionando? ¿Qué tipo de fallas podrían ocurrir para hacer que las cosas que están funcionando dejen de funcionar? Comente otras formas de energía que estuvieron disponibles durante la falla eléctrica. Tal vez usted tenía velas o una linterna de pilas, además de la energía solar.

Destrezas del proceso científico

La destreza de **predecir** requiere que los estudiantes anticipen resultados de sucesos futuros basados en patrones de experiencia.

Use una pelota de goma para comentar la energía potencial y cinética. Pregunte a su hijo(a) si la pelota tiene o no energía cuando está en el suelo. Luego ruede la pelota y pregúntele: ¿De dónde proviene la energía? (Su cuerpo proporcionó la energía para poner la pelota en movimiento.)

Coloque la pelota en el borde de una mesa o sobre un mostrador. Pregúntele nuevamente si la pelota tiene energía (Ésta tiene energía potencial.) Deje caer la pelota desde el borde y que rebote. (La pelota muestra la energía cinética cuando está en movimiento.)

Comente con su hijo(a) la idea de energía potencial, la energía que tiene un objeto es debido al lugar donde se encuentra o a su condición. Coloque la pelota en diferentes lugares y hable sobre si su energía potencial aumentará o disminuirá en cada situación. (Mientras más alta está la pelota, ésta tiene más energía potencial.) Pida a su hijo(a) que prediga dónde se podría colocar la pelota para un máximo de energía potencial.

Materiales de casa para la actividad

Querido familiar:

Para hacer las actividades en este capítulo, necesitaremos algunos materiales que tal vez tenga en la casa. Observe los artículos de la lista de la derecha. Si es posible, por favor envíe estas cosas con su hijo(a) a la escuela.

¡Gracias por su ayuda y su apoyo!

____ **pelota de tenis**
____ **cartulina ondulada de 12 pulg por 12 pulg**
____ **espejo pequeño**
____ **cuchillo de metal para untar mantequilla**
____ **vasos de estireno**
____ **cuchillos de plástico**

Harcourt

School-Home Connection

Chapter Content

Our science class is beginning a chapter about how people use energy. Ask your child to list and define the various sources and uses of energy explored in this chapter. What are the energy sources used in your community or larger area? Together, visit your local library and research an energy source other than the burning of fossil fuels.

ScienceFun

Using pencil and paper, work with your child to design a machine that would convert a source of energy that you already have available into electricity to light your home or run your appliances. Be imaginative. For example, if someone in your house works out on an exercise machine, think of how you could attach the machine to a generator. Other ideas might be to hook up a generator to a hamster's exercise wheel, attach a wind turbine to the top of your house or apartment building, or to install solar panels on your roof. Draw your ideas in the space at the right.

Science Process Skills

The skill of observing involves using one or more of the senses to perceive properties through the use of simple or complex instruments. The skill of **measuring** involves making quantitative observations using both non-standard and standard measures.

Take a meter tour of your home. With your child, look at your electric meter and your gas meter and discuss what is being measured. Look at your thermostat and discuss what it measures. If you have an oil tank, look at the gauge that shows how full the tank is. Ask your child to suggest reasons for having all these ways of measuring energy and fuel.

My Electricity Maker

Activity Materials from Home

Dear Family Member:

To do the activities in this chapter, we will need some materials that you may have around your home. Please note the items at the right. If possible, please send these things to school with your child.

Your help and support are appreciated!

____ four 10-cm plastic disks (of the sort used to cover coffee cans and large yogurt containers)
____ plastic basin
____ 1-liter plastic bottle

Harcourt

La escuela y la casa

Harcourt Ciencias

Contenido del capítulo

Nuestra clase de ciencias comienza un capítulo sobre cómo usamos la energía. Pida a su hijo(a) que enumere y defina los diferentes usos y fuentes de energía que se exploran en este capítulo. ¿Cuáles son las fuentes de energía que se usan en tu comunidad o un área más grande? Juntos, visiten la biblioteca local e investiguen una fuente de energía excepto la quema de combustibles de fósiles.

Diversión

Trabaje con su hijo(a), usando lápiz y papel, para diseñar una máquina que podría convertir una fuente de energía que ya está disponible en electricidad, para alumbrar tu casa o hacer funcionar los artefactos. Sé creativo. Por ejemplo, si alguien en tu casa hace ejercicios en una máquina de ejercicios, piensa en cómo podrías conectar la máquina a un generador. Otras ideas podrían ser conectar un generador a una rueda para hámsters, conectar una turbina de viento al techo de tu casa o apartamento o instalar paneles solares en tu techo. Anota tus ideas en el espacio de la derecha.

Destrezas del proceso científico

La destreza de observar involucra el uso de uno o más sentidos para percibir las propiedades a través del uso de instrumentos sencillos o complejos. La destreza de **medir** involucra hacer observaciones cuantitativas usando medidas estándar y no estándar.

Con su hijo(a) mire el medidor eléctrico y el de gas y comenten lo que se mide. Mire su termostato y comente lo que mide. Si su calefacción funciona con aceite, revise el indicador que muestra hasta dónde está lleno el tanque. Pida a su hijo(a) que sugiera las razones de tener todas estas formas de medir energía y combustible.

Mi productor de electricidad

Materiales de casa para la actividad

Querido familiar:

Para hacer las actividades en este capítulo, necesitaremos algunos materiales que tal vez tenga en la casa. Observe los artículos de la lista de la derecha. Si es posible, por favor envíe estas cosas con su hijo(a) a la escuela.

¡Gracias por su ayuda y su apoyo!

_____ **cuatro tapas de 10 cm (del tipo usado para cubrir latas de café y recipientes grandes de yogur)**
_____ **tazón de plástico**
_____ **botella de plástico de 1 litro**

Harcourt

Participating
in a
School Science Fair
by Barry Van Deman

Science Fair Success

Science fairs can be rewarding or frustrating for teachers, parents, and students. The key to success is deciding on the desired outcomes and planning accordingly. When a science fair turns out badly, it is usually because there is confusion about expectations for student projects. The result is a hodgepodge of projects–everything from volcano models and posters of dolphins to demonstrations and experiments. Judging these disparate projects often results in confused judges, disappointed students, and disgruntled parents.

First Step — Project Categories

The first step for science fair success is to decide the outcome you expect for students and what kinds of projects will lead them there. Projects usually fall into one of the following four categories:

Poster Displays

Students draw or cut and paste pictures on posters. They select a topic, such as dolphins, dogs, or space, and read about it so that they are able to explain to others what they have learned. An outcome for students is that they learn about a science topic.

Models

Students make models of, for example, a volcano, the solar system, or a bridge. They might make poster displays to accompany their models, and they might demonstrate how the models work. Outcomes for students include learning about a science topic and gaining skill in constructing models.

Demonstrations

Students perform a science demonstration, such as mixing baking soda and vinegar to demonstrate a chemical reaction. They might make poster displays to illustrate the demonstrations. Outcomes for students include learning about a science topic and gaining practice in using science process skills.

Experiments

Students conduct a controlled experiment, such as testing the effects of plant food on potted plants. They usually make poster displays to show the stages of their experiments. Since experiments involve using many science process skills, an outcome for students is that they grow in their understanding of scientific methods.

One way to eliminate confusion for all is to limit students to only one category of projects. If projects are to be judged, judging criteria should align with the project category. That is, criteria for projects that involve models should differ from criteria used to judge experiments.

While projects in any of the categories provide valuable experiences for students, projects that involve experiments help them understand scientific methods and develop multiple process skills. In the pages that follow, this guide will focus on experimental projects.

Second Step–Communication

The second step to science fair success is to communicate your expectations to students and to their parents or guardians. A letter you can send to parents at the start of the project is included in the following pages. It will help parents to know how to guide their children without doing the projects for them. Be sure to keep parents informed as preparation for the science fair continues.

Science Fair Project Ideas

Working on science fair projects can help your students gain experience in applying the scientific methods and science process skills learned through their interaction with *Harcourt Science*.

For additional ideas for Science Fair Projects see pages A1, B1, C1, D1, E1, and F1 in your *Harcourt Science* Teacher Edition. Unit Experiment prompts found on these pages are further explained on pages A1i, A1j, B1i, B1j, C1i, C1j, D1i, D1j, E1i, E1j, F1i, and F1j of your *Harcourt Science* Teacher Edition.

Science Fair: School-Home Connection

Dear Parent or Guardian,

We will be holding our school science fair on _____. Participating in a science fair is an enjoyable way for students to learn how to conduct experiments to solve problems. Students will make displays that show how they went about conducting their experiments.

This science fair is not quite like the science fairs you may have experienced. While models and modeling are important to science, we are not encouraging students to display models of such things as volcanoes and the solar system. Instead, we are encouraging them to ask questions and then to set up experiments to answer those questions. In this way, they learn to approach science as scientists do.

I will be sending home more information from time to time, but in the meantime, I would like to suggest how you might support your child's progress on his or her project.

- Talk to your son or daughter about what he or she might be interested in finding out. Work together to formulate a question that can be answered by setting up an experiment.
- Take your son or daughter to the library or help him or her search online for information about the topic.
- Help your son or daughter think about an experiment that would help answer the project question.
- Help gather the materials necessary to conduct the experiment. Observe and ask questions as your son or daughter carries out the experiment, but be careful not to conduct the experiment or draw conclusions.
- Help with gathering materials for the project display. Allow your son or daughter to make the display with only some help from you.

Obviously, we want the projects to be done by the students and not by their parents, but this can be a good time for parent and child to work together. If you have any questions, please contact me.

Sincerely,

Harcourt

Science Fair Project Timeline

Date of the Science Fair _____

Date Due	Date Completed	Things to Do
		Choose a topic and write a project question.
		Research the topic using books, the Internet, and other resources.
		Write a hypothesis.
		Design an experiment to test the hypothesis.
		Conduct the experiment and record observations.
		Make a table, or chart, for data. Draw one or more graphs of the data.
		Write the project report.
		Make the project display, or exhibit.
		Present the project at the science fair.
		Other:

Harcourt

Making Your Project Display

Your project display will communicate to others what your project is all about. The display is three-sided and has a brief description of the various parts of your investigation. You can make your display from poster board, or use a ready-made project display board. The pages that follow offer you an outline for a summary for your project display and a guide to writing a longer project report.

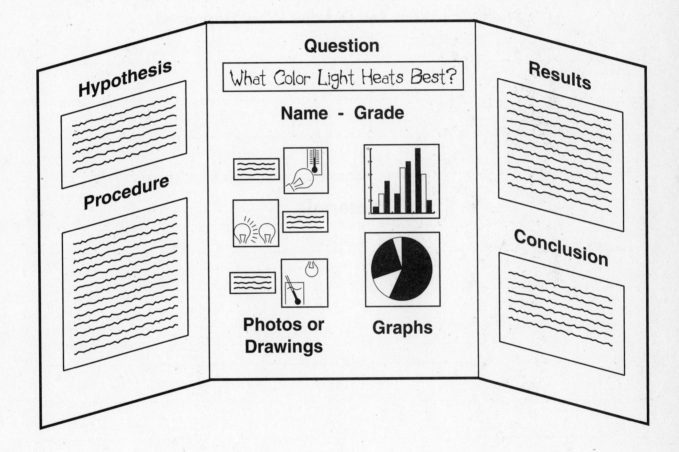

Hypothesis

Procedure

Question

What Color Light Heats Best?

Name - Grade

Photos or Drawings

Graphs

Results

Conclusion

Harcourt

Name _____ Date _____

Display Summary

Project Question/Title

_____

_____

Project Description
Briefly Tell What You Did and What Happened

_____

_____

_____

_____

Materials

_____   _____

_____   _____

_____   _____

_____   _____

Procedure

_____

_____

_____

_____

Continue your procedure on additional sheets of paper, if necessary.

Harcourt

Observations

Include a brief written summary of observations. You will want to make large, colorful displays of graphs of any data you collected.

_____

_____

_____

_____

Conclusions

_____

_____

_____

_____

_____

_____

Suggestions for Follow-Up Experiments

_____

_____

_____

_____

_____

Harcourt

Writing Your Science Fair Project Report

Your project report communicates to others how you did your experiment and what you found out from it. This is where you use your notes and observations from your experiment.

An Outline for Your Project Report

1. **Cover Page** — In the upper middle of the paper, write the title of your project or your project question. Also include your name on the cover page.

2. **Project Question** — Begin your report by stating your project question.

3. **Hypothesis** — State your hypothesis.

4. **Research** — Write about what you found out from books, the Web, and other resources that helped you design an experiment and answer your project question.

5. **Experiment Plan** — Describe the design for your experiment. Be sure to describe the variables and how you set up a fair test.

6. **Procedure** — Describe how you carried out your experiment and what you found out.

7. **Present Data** — Include your data tables and graphs.

8. **Conclusions** — Compare your results to your hypothesis. Did your findings support your hypothesis or not?

9. **Bibliography** — Write your bibliography. A bibliography includes the names of books, magazines, web sites, and other resources you used for your project.

Writing Models

The writing models on the following pages show examples of writing for different purposes. Students can consult these as they complete the Writing Links described in the *Harcourt Science* Pupil Edition or other writing assignments described in the Teacher's Edition. You may wish to distribute copies of the writing models to students or display them on an overhead transparency.

Informative Writing

Persuasive Writing

Narrative Writing

Expressive Writing

Harcourt

Writing in Science

Model: How-To Writing

How-to writing gives directions or explains how to do something. Steps are given in time order.

topic sentence

materials needed

time-order words in steps

How to Grow a Plant

It's easy to grow a plant from a seed. To get started, you'll need a small plant pot and tray, a bag of potting soil, one or two large seeds, and a container of water.

First, place the tray under the pot. Then carefully fill the pot with soil. Pat the soil down lightly to make it firm. Use your finger to poke a hole about $\frac{1}{2}$ inch deep in the soil. Next, put the seed in the hole. Cover the seed with soil. Then water the soil until it is moist but not muddy. Set the pot near a sunny window. Water the soil every few days. In a few days, you will see a green shoot coming out of the soil. That means that the seed has germinated. Your plant will begin to grow. Water the little plant every day to keep the soil moist.

Harcourt

Writing in Science

Model: Classification

In a **classification essay**, a writer shows how things can be grouped into categories. Often, examples of each category are provided.

title	**Different Types of Resources**
topic sentence	Natural resources can be divided into three categories: nonrenewable, renewable, and reusable resources.
first category defined	Nonrenewable resources cannot be replaced in one lifetime after they are used up. Rock and mineral resources, such as coal, silicon, copper, and iron are nonrenewable resources. Oil is another nonrenewable resource.
second category defined	Renewable resources are resources that can be replaced as they are used. Forests are an example of a renewable resource. When full-grown trees are cut down to make paper and lumber, new trees can be planted to replace them.
third category defined	Reusable resources can be used over and over again. Air and water are good examples of reusable resources. It is important to remember that these resources are only reusable if people are careful. If air and water get polluted, they can become unusable.

Writing in Science

Model: Research Report

A **research report** provides information about a topic. Reports can be short, or they can be several pages long.

title	**The Galveston Hurricane**
introduction that identifies topic	The worst natural disaster in United States history was the Galveston, Texas hurricane of 1900. It helped people realize the importance of being prepared for storms.
body with detailed information about topic	The hurricane struck Galveston, a low coastal island, on September 8. Forecasters warned that severe weather was coming, but many people ignored or did not hear the warnings. Winds rose to an estimated 120 miles per hour. Huge waves swept over the city. Some survivors drifted for hours on pieces of lumber from shattered buildings. Others were not so lucky. By the time the storm ended, more than 8,000 people had lost their lives.
conclusion	The hurricane proved how important it was to be prepared for storms. After the hurricane, the citizens of Galveston built a sea wall to prevent future disasters. Meteorologists worked harder than ever to predict hurricanes and warn people about them.

Harcourt

Writing in Science

Model: Narration

A **narration** presents events in the order in which they occurred. Often, a narration is an eyewitness account of those events.

title	**Sunlight and Plant Growth**
introduction **topic sentence**	Any science book will tell you that plants need sunlight to grow. Our science discovery team thinks that seeing is believing. That's why we did an experiment to show how sunlight affects plant growth.
events described in time order	The first thing we did was to choose three pea plants. Each plant was 3 cm high. Plant "A" was placed by a window. In that spot it would receive more than six hours of sunlight each day. Plant "B" was placed by the window for three hours each day. After that it was placed in a covered box for the rest of the day. Plant "C" was kept in a covered box all day. Each plant was given 250 mL of water every three days.
conclusion	We followed this plan for two weeks. After that the plants were measured again. Plant "A" had grown 12 cm. Plant "B" had grown 5 cm. Plant "C" had grown less than 2 cm. Our results were clear. Sunlight helps plants to grow.

Writing in Science

Model: Explanation

In an **explanation**, the writer helps the reader understand something, such as what something is, how it works, what happens during a process, or why something happens.

title	**How Water Changes State**
topic sentence	Water can be in any one of the three states of matter. It can be a solid, a liquid, and a gas. When heat is added or removed, water can change state.
body/detailed explanation	At temperatures at or below 0°C, water is in its solid state. The particles that make it up are packed closely together and move very little. Solid water, or ice, has a definite volume and shape.
	When solid water is heated to above 0°C, it changes to its liquid state. In liquid water, the particles move easily enough to slide past each other. When liquid water is cooled to 0°C, it changes back to its solid state.
	When water is heated to 100°C, it boils and changes to a gas called water vapor. The particles in the water vapor are far apart and move fast. When water vapor is cooled it condenses, or turns to liquid.

Writing in Science

Model: Compare/Contrast

In a **compare-and-contrast essay**, a writer shows how two people, places, or things are alike and how they are different.

title	**Deer and Whales**
topic sentence **likenesses**	It may not seem like it at first, but the white-tailed deer and the blue whale are alike in many ways. Both animals are warm-blooded. Both animals keep their young close by when they are small. Both the deer and the blue whale breath air into their lungs. Both animals must forage for food to survive.
topic sentence **differences**	Even though they are both mammals, the white-tailed deer and the blue whale are very different. The deer is a land animal. It walks on four legs, and eats plants such as grasses, twigs, and leaves. The whale is a water animal. It swims using its powerful flippers and tail. It feeds on tiny shrimp-like sea creatures called krill. The deer usually stays within a small territory. The blue whale may travel thousands of miles as it migrates each year.

Writing in Science

Model: Description

A **description** creates a word picture as it tells about one subject. It has a beginning, a middle, and an ending. It includes sensory details.

title	**The Avalanche**
beginning that tells what you will describe	The snow-covered mountains looked like a peaceful postcard. But in a matter of seconds, the beautiful scene changed to a picture of terror.
middle with sensory details	With a boom that echoed through the valley, a wall of snow began to tumble down the mountain. In an instant, the potential energy in the snow was transformed into kinetic energy. The avalanche quickly grew larger as it roared down the mountain's rocky face. Trees, boulders, and even buildings disappeared under the gigantic wave of snow.
ending	In less than two minutes, the avalanche was over. The energy of the avalanche was lost, as sound and as heat from the friction of the moving snow. Then all was still.

Harcourt

Writing in Science

Model: Opinion

An **opinion** essay has a beginning, a middle with paragraphs supporting the writer's opinion, and an ending.

title	**Protect Animal Habitats**
beginning with opinion stated	Many threatened and endangered species are fighting to avoid extinction. I think the best way to protect them is to protect their habitats from damage by humans.
middle with reasons to support opinion	Human damage to animal habitats puts many species in danger. Each year, humans destroy millions of acres of wild lands to build new roads, homes, and businesses. This takes away the land where animals used to live. In addition, humans often pollute natural habitats. This makes them unfit for use by plants and animals. Humans also damage habitats by bringing in new species that prove harmful to animal populations that are already there.
ending with restated opinion or request for action	If we are more careful about the way we use land, we will do less damage to habitats. With healthy habitats to live in, endangered and threatened species will be able to survive.

Harcourt

Writing in Science

Model: Request

To **request** information or products from a company, use a business-letter format. A business letter has the same parts as a friendly letter, plus an inside address. It also uses formal language.

heading

15 Main Street
Worcester, VT 05682
July 15, 2001

inside address

Mr. Jacob Lee
313 Hollis Street
Montpelier, VT 05602

greeting

Dear Mr. Lee:

statement of request and supporting reasons

The Worcester Mountain Club will be taking its annual endangered plant survey on September 3. I would like to invite you to help in this effort.

Before we can protect the endangered plants in the Worcester Range, we must identify them. We cannot do this without the help of volunteers.

Over the years, people from across Vermont have helped us with our survey. Their hard work has paid off. Last Labor Day, we discovered three species never before seen in the Worcester Range.

We look forward to another fun survey day this September 3. Won't you please join us? We will meet at the Worcester Mountain House, 15 Elmore Road, at 9 A.M.

closing

Sincerely,

signature

Suzanne Hollister

Harcourt

Writing in Science

Model: Business Letter

In a **business letter** a writer uses formal language to ask for or share information, to request something, or to praise or complain about a product or service. It has the same parts as a friendly letter, plus an inside address.

heading

9 Bennett St.
Eldred, PA 16731
September 15, 2002

inside address

Ms. Eleanor Nucci
Corning Museum of Glass
One Museum Way
Corning, NY 14830

greeting

Dear Ms. Nucci:

Our fifth-grade class at Eldred Elementary School would like to thank you for the personal tour of the Corning Museum of Glass. We really appreciate that you took the time to answer all of our questions. We all learned a lot about how glass is made and used.

body

Since returning to our school, we have begun to research how glass is used in the computer industry. And we have also begun a glass recycling program at our school. We thought you would be glad to hear that!

Thank you again for your informative tour.

closing

Sincerely,

signature

James Paige

Harcourt

Writing in Science

Model: Story

Every **story** has a setting (time and place), one or more characters, and a series of events called a plot. A plot has a beginning, a middle, and an end.

title	**The Discovery**
beginning: introduce the setting and the characters	Dr. Andrea Shaughnessey began her day as she usually did. She put on her oxygen tank and mask, so she could breathe outdoors without choking on the black, polluted air.
middle: a plot with a problem to solve	As she walked to her laboratory, she wondered how the pollution had gotten so bad. If only people had listened to the warnings. But now it was too late—unless her experiment was a success. She had worked for ten years to build a machine that filtered pollutants from the atmosphere. The results of the test run would arrive this morning.
	"Wouldn't it be great," she thought, "if people could stop to smell the roses again? Well, first we'd have to grow some roses since they haven't been able to survive with so little sunlight. But *then*, people could stop to smell them!"
end: the problem is solved	When Andrea reached the lab, she didn't have to guess the test results. The other scientists on her team welcomed her with a cheer! They had received an e-mail from the space agency that morning. The machine worked even better than they had hoped. Everyone could breath a sigh of relief. Andrea was a hero!

Writing in Science

Model: Personal Story

A **personal story** is told in the first person. Someone or something is telling the story, using pronouns such as *I, my,* and *me.* Like any story, there is a beginning, a middle, and an end.

title	**Wetlands Surprise**
beginning: the narrator is identified	When my father told me we would visit the Callard Creek Wetland, I wasn't too excited. To me, a wetland was nothing more than a boring old swamp. "You're in for a surprise," Dad said, but I didn't believe him. Was I ever wrong!
middle: the narrator tells a series of events	By the time the sun rose, we had paddled our canoe half a mile out into the wetland. Suddenly, the world around us exploded with life. Flocks of snow geese spread their wings and took flight. Tall, regal herons fished along the edges of the weed beds. Muskrats and turtles swam so close to our canoe, I could almost touch them. The whole day was filled with incredible sights and sounds.
end: the narrator wraps up the story	On the way home, Dad asked me if I had been too bored by the "old swamp." I just smiled, knowing I would return to Callard Creek again and again.

Writing in Science

A **poem** uses rhythm and language that appeals to the senses to paint a "word picture" for the reader. Some poems have rhyming lines, but some poems do not.

title	Hibernation
"word pictures" that help the reader picture what the poem is about	My body has stored its winter fat. Even the sun is cold. The geese have flown. The night has painted Sheets of ice upon the rivers. It is time for the long sleep.

Harcourt

Writing in Science

Model: Friendly Letter

In a **friendly letter**, a person writes to someone he or she knows. A friendly letter has a heading, a greeting, a body, a closing, and a signature. In the heading, include a comma between the city and state, and between the day of the month and the year.

heading (writer's address and date)

2214 Westgate Drive
St. Paul, MN 55114
August 10, 2001

greeting

Dear Andrew,

    I hope you are having fun since you got back from space camp. It was cool to learn about the space stations and the different kinds of space probes. I loved building our own rocket too. Even though our rocket didn't go the highest, I think it was the best. We made an excellent engineering team.

body

    Have you gotten your new telescope yet? Mom and Dad say I can have one, but I have to earn some of the money myself. I guess that means I'll be starting out with something a little smaller than the Hubble telescope we learned about!

    When we both get our telescopes, maybe you can come and visit me for a night of star gazing. Until then, keep your eye on the sky. Write me back when you have any news.

closing

Your friend,

signature

Luis

Harcourt

ACTIVITIES FOR HOME OR SCHOOL

BALLOON LUNGS

How do lungs work?

Materials
- 2 balloons
- plastic soda bottle
- scissors

Procedure
1. Remove the cap and cut the bottom off the bottle.
2. Put one balloon into the bottle. Secure the lip of the balloon to the top of the bottle.

3. Cut the lip off the second balloon. Stretch the large part of the second balloon over the bottom of the bottle.
4. With your fingers, pull down on the second balloon and then release it. Observe what happens to the first balloon.

Draw Conclusions
When you pull on the second balloon, what happens inside the bottle? What part of the respiratory system does each part of your model represent?

SKELETAL SYSTEMS

What adaptations do skeletons show?

Materials
- butcher paper
- meterstick
- 5 people
- marker

Procedure
1. Measure out about 7 m of butcher paper.
2. Have one person lie in the center of the paper. This person should stretch out his or her arms as shown.
3. Have two other people lie end-to-end on each side of the first person.

4. Use the marker to draw around the first person, including the top edge of his or her outstretched arms and thumbs.
5. To complete the top edge, draw a sloping line the lengths of the people on both sides as shown. Draw the lower edge with four points and four scallops as shown.

Draw Conclusions
While the skeletal systems of all mammals are similar, there are differences due to various adaptations. The skeletons of bats show adaptations for flight. If humans could fly, how many times longer than their bodies would their wings need to be? What other skeletal adaptations of mammals can you think of?

A31

Harcourt

Name _____ Date _____

ACTIVITIES FOR HOME OR SCHOOL

BACKBONE CONSTRUCTION

How do backbones give vertebrates flexible support?

Materials
- construction paper
- tape
- scissors
- book

Procedure

❶ Roll the paper into a tube about 5 cm across. Tape all along the edge.

❷ Stand the tube on one end. Will the tube hold up a pair of scissors? A book? More than one book?

❸ Squeeze the tube gently to make an oval. Make slits about 2 cm apart all down the tube. Cut the slits from each side almost to the middle.

❹ Experiment to see how much weight the tube will now hold up.

Draw Conclusions

What happened each time the tube gave way? How did the cuts change the tube?

PLANTS AND WATER

Why do leaves give off water?

Materials
- pencil
- water
- marker
- scissors
- piece of thin cardboard
- leaf with a long stem
- modeling clay
- 2 clear plastic cups

Procedure

❶ Carefully use the pencil to poke a hole in the center of the cardboard. Then push the leaf stem through the hole. Use the clay to close up the hole around the stem. Be careful not to pinch the stem.

❷ Fill one cup about $\frac{2}{3}$ full with water. Mark the water line with the marker.

❸ Snip off about 1 cm from the stem end. Place the cut stem into the water, resting the cardboard on the rim of the cup. Place the empty cup over the leaf. Set the cups in the sun.

❹ After a few hours, observe both cups and the stem. Record your observations.

Draw Conclusions

What can you infer from your observations?

A57

Harcourt

Name _____ Date _____

DNA

How does DNA fit into a cell?

Materials
- sewing thread
- meterstick
- gelatin capsule

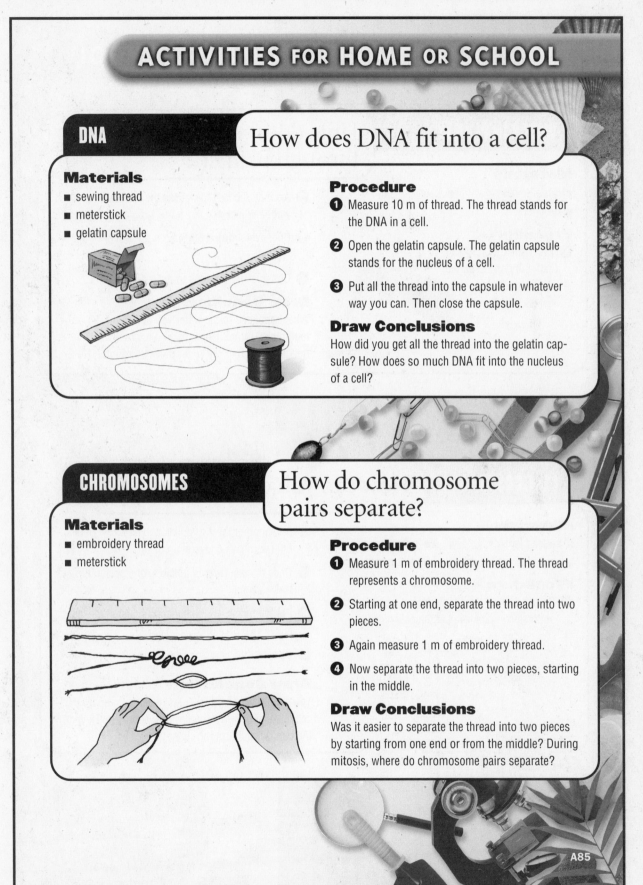

Procedure

❶ Measure 10 m of thread. The thread stands for the DNA in a cell.

❷ Open the gelatin capsule. The gelatin capsule stands for the nucleus of a cell.

❸ Put all the thread into the capsule in whatever way you can. Then close the capsule.

Draw Conclusions

How did you get all the thread into the gelatin capsule? How does so much DNA fit into the nucleus of a cell?

CHROMOSOMES

How do chromosome pairs separate?

Materials
- embroidery thread
- meterstick

Procedure

❶ Measure 1 m of embroidery thread. The thread represents a chromosome.

❷ Starting at one end, separate the thread into two pieces.

❸ Again measure 1 m of embroidery thread.

❹ Now separate the thread into two pieces, starting in the middle.

Draw Conclusions

Was it easier to separate the thread into two pieces by starting from one end or from the middle? During mitosis, where do chromosome pairs separate?

A85

Use with page A85.

Harcourt

ACTIVITIES FOR HOME OR SCHOOL

WATER IN PLANTS

How does water move through plants?

Materials
- 5 toothpicks
- water
- dropper

Procedure

❶ Break the toothpicks in half, but don't separate the parts. The two halves should remain connected.

❷ Arrange the toothpicks like the spokes in a wagon wheel.

❸ Put several drops of water in the center of the "wheel."

❹ Observe any changes to the toothpicks.

Draw Conclusions

What happened to the water you put on the toothpicks? What happened to the toothpicks? Relate this to the way water moves through plants.

LEAF CASTS

How can you observe stomata?

Materials
- potted plant
- clear fingernail polish
- microscope slide
- microscope

Procedure

❶ Paint a 2-cm square of fingernail polish on the underside of one leaf. Let the polish dry.

❷ Add another layer of polish and let it dry. Repeat until you have 6 layers of polish.

❸ Once the last layer of polish is dry, peel it off the leaf.

❹ Put the polish, which contains a cast of the leaf epidermis, on a microscope slide.

❺ Observe the slide by using the microscope.

Draw Conclusions

You should observe two types of cells. Compare the cells. Explain any differences between them. How do the guard cells form the stomata?

A117

Harcourt

Name _____   Date _____

THE CARBON CYCLE

Where can you find carbon?

Materials
- candle
- match
- aluminum pie pan
- white paper
- charcoal
- pencil
- hand lens

Procedure

1. Your teacher or another adult will light the candle and hold it under the aluminum pie pan for a few seconds.

2. Observe the black soot that forms on the pan.

3. After the pan cools, use your finger to scrape off some of the soot. Wipe your finger on the white paper.

4. Now rub the charcoal on the paper. Then make several marks on the paper with the pencil.

5. Using the hand lens, compare the materials on the paper.

Draw Conclusions

What material is in the soot, the charcoal, and the pencil? How did this material become part of each? Where else can you find this material?

THE WATER CYCLE

What are the parts of the water cycle?

Materials
- safety goggles
- 500-mL beaker
- water
- hot plate
- hot pad
- tongs
- glass plate

Procedure

1. **CAUTION** Put on the safety goggles. Put about 400 mL of water in the beaker.

2. Heat the beaker on the hot plate until the water starts to boil.

3. Using the hot pad and the tongs, your teacher or another adult will hold the glass plate above the beaker to catch the steam.

4. Observe the water drops that form on the glass plate and fall back into the beaker.

Draw Conclusions

Where in the model were evaporation, condensation, and precipitation taking place? Heat from the hot plate caused the water to boil. What heat source causes evaporation in nature?

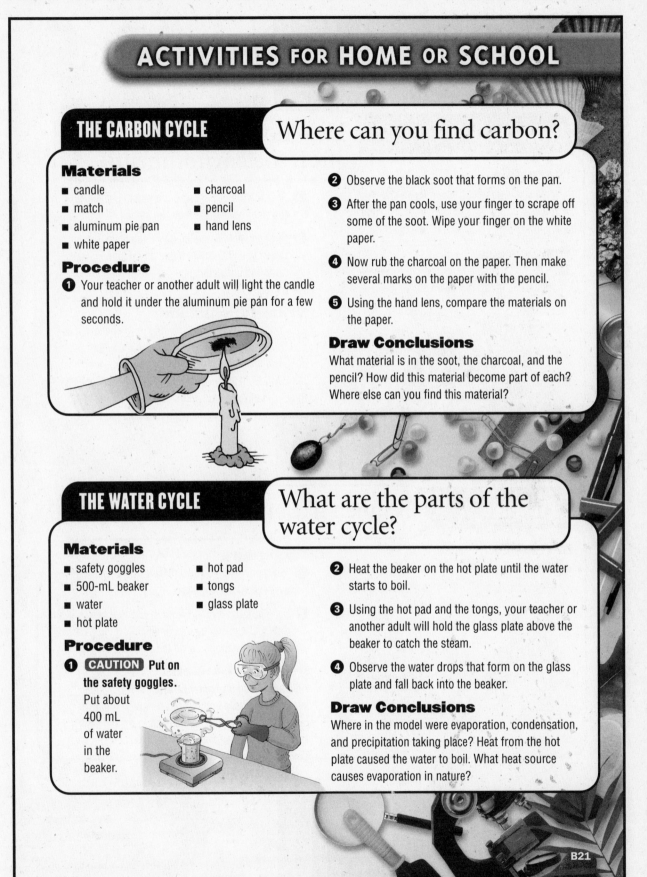

B21

Harcourt

Use with page B21.

Name _____ Date _____

ACTIVITIES FOR HOME OR SCHOOL

FEAST ON THIS!

How does an animal's diet affect the environment?

Materials
- sanitized owl pellet
- forceps
- toothpicks
- hand lens
- black paper
- glue

Procedure
1. Use the forceps and toothpicks to separate the materials in the owl pellet.

2. Sort the materials using the hand lens. Group together bones that look the same.

3. Reconstruct the skeletons on the black paper. When you are satisfied that all the bones are arranged correctly, glue the skeletons to the paper.

Draw Conclusions
How many skeletons did you find in the pellet? If an owl throws up one pellet a day, how many animals does the owl eat in a year? If all the owls were removed from an ecosystem, what would happen to the population of prey animals?

PYRAMIDS

Is lunch like an energy pyramid?

Materials
- food-guide pyramid
- energy pyramid

Procedure
1. Put the food-guide pyramid next to the energy pyramid. Compare them.

2. Look at today's menu from the school cafeteria. See if it also makes a pyramid according to the recommendations of the food-guide pyramid.

Draw Conclusions
How are the energy pyramid and the food-guide pyramid alike? Does the cafeteria menu meet the recommendations of the food-guide pyramid? What level consumers are people?

B57

Harcourt

ACTIVITIES FOR HOME OR SCHOOL

LAND BIOMES

What adaptations do animals from land biomes show?

Materials
- terrarium
- bedding
- water bottle
- food
- small animal: hamster, mouse, snake, or lizard

Procedure
1. Set up the terrarium to meet the needs of the animal.
2. Observe the animal in this environment for several days.

Draw Conclusions
What needs of the animal did you provide? What adaptations does the animal have for living in a land biome? What is the natural environment of the animal? How does the terrarium compare to the natural environment?

WATER ECOSYSTEMS

What interactions occur in water ecosystems?

Materials
- bucket
- collecting net
- large jar or aquarium
- air pump

Procedure
1. With an adult, visit a stream or pond in your community.
2. Use the bucket and the collecting net to scoop up sand, water, water plants, and water animals.
3. Transfer the materials and organisms to the jar or aquarium.
4. Set up the air pump, and observe the water ecosystem.

Draw Conclusions
List all the living and nonliving things in the ecosystem. How do the living things interact with each other? How do the living things and nonliving things interact?

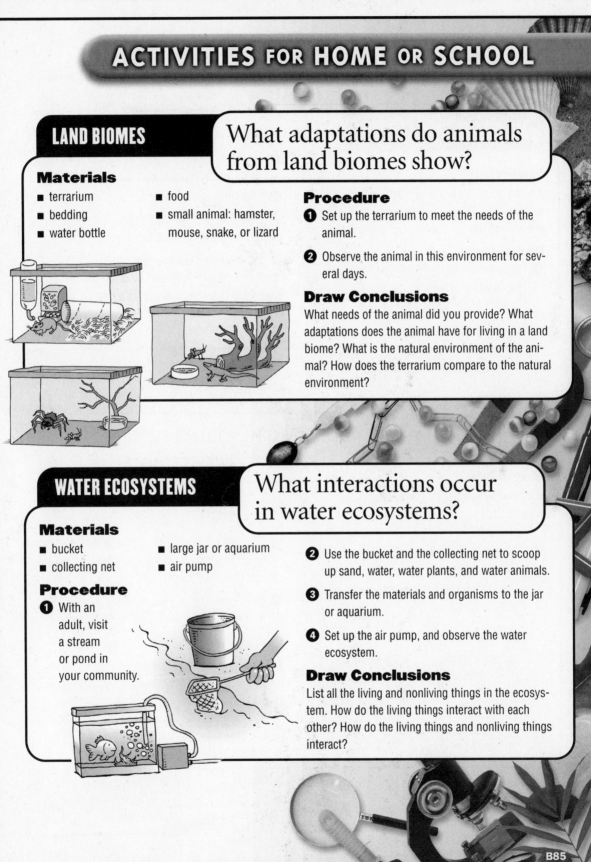

Harcourt

B85

Name _____ Date _____

ACID RAIN

How does acid rain affect art objects?

Materials

- chalk
- paper clip
- modeling clay
- vinegar
- dropper

Procedure

1. Using the paper clip as a tool, carve the piece of chalk into a sculpture.

2. Place your sculpture on a base of clay.

3. Using the dropper, drop vinegar onto your sculpture and observe what happens.

Draw Conclusions

What effect does the vinegar, an acid, have on your sculpture? Chalk is similar to the limestone and marble of real art objects. What do you infer is happening to art objects around the world because of acid rain?

POWERFUL PLANTS

How can plants reclaim a damaged ecosystem?

Materials

- 2 small clay pots
- potting soil
- 6 bean seeds
- water
- flour

Procedure

1. Fill both pots half-full of soil. Plant three bean seeds in each pot, and water them with equal amounts of water.

2. Mix the flour and water until it forms a thick batter.

3. Pour the batter into one pot, covering the soil and completely filling the space between the soil and the top of the pot.

4. Place both pots in a warm, sunny place. Water the soil of the uncovered pot when it feels dry.

5. Observe the pots every day for two weeks.

Draw Conclusions

Which pot is the control? What do you observe about the plants in the experimental pot? Where have you noticed plants growing in similar conditions in your neighborhood? How do plants help reclaim damaged ecosystems?

B117

Harcourt

Use with page B117.

Name _____ Date _____

MODEL EARTH — How can you model Earth's layers?

Materials
- rounded objects, such as
  - an apple
  - an avocado
  - a peach
  - a hard-boiled egg
  - a nectarine
  - a tennis ball
  - an orange
  - a plum
  - plain chocolates, or chocolate-covered peanuts

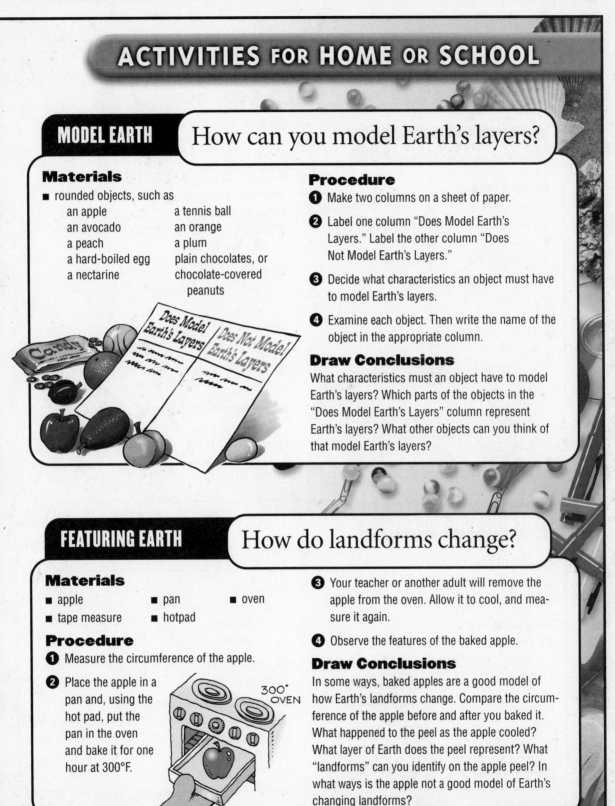

Procedure

❶ Make two columns on a sheet of paper.

❷ Label one column "Does Model Earth's Layers." Label the other column "Does Not Model Earth's Layers."

❸ Decide what characteristics an object must have to model Earth's layers.

❹ Examine each object. Then write the name of the object in the appropriate column.

Draw Conclusions

What characteristics must an object have to model Earth's layers? Which parts of the objects in the "Does Model Earth's Layers" column represent Earth's layers? What other objects can you think of that model Earth's layers?

FEATURING EARTH — How do landforms change?

Materials
- apple
- tape measure
- pan
- hotpad
- oven

Procedure

❶ Measure the circumference of the apple.

❷ Place the apple in a pan and, using the hot pad, put the pan in the oven and bake it for one hour at 300°F.

300° OVEN

❸ Your teacher or another adult will remove the apple from the oven. Allow it to cool, and measure it again.

❹ Observe the features of the baked apple.

Draw Conclusions

In some ways, baked apples are a good model of how Earth's landforms change. Compare the circumference of the apple before and after you baked it. What happened to the peel as the apple cooled? What layer of Earth does the peel represent? What "landforms" can you identify on the apple peel? In what ways is the apple not a good model of Earth's changing landforms?

C29

Harcourt

ACTIVITIES FOR HOME OR SCHOOL

GROWING CRYSTALS

How are minerals left behind by evaporation?

Materials

- plastic gloves
- safety goggles
- apron
- 1 tablespoon of laundry bluing
- 1 tablespoon of water
- 1 tablespoon of ammonia
- 1 tablespoon of table salt
- plastic cup
- spoon
- sponge
- plastic bowl
- food coloring

Procedure

CAUTION Be sure to wear gloves, safety goggles, and an apron.

❶ Mix the bluing, water, ammonia, and salt in the plastic cup. Stir gently until the salt has dissolved.

❷ Place the sponge in the bowl. Pour the mixture over the sponge. Throw away the cup.

❸ Sprinkle 4 drops of food coloring over the sponge. Wait one day.

Draw Conclusions

Observe the sponge. Does it change? What is forming?

WEATHERING ROCK

How can you model weathering by using chalk?

Materials

- 2 pieces of chalk
- plastic jar with lid
- water
- strainer

Procedure

❶ Break each piece of chalk into about three pieces. Put all the chalk pieces except one into the jar.

❷ Pour water into the jar until the chalk is covered. Put the lid on the jar. Make sure it is tightly sealed. Shake the jar for about 5 minutes to "weather" the chalk.

❸ Pour the water through the strainer to get the chalk pieces.

Draw Conclusions

Compare the strained pieces to the chalk that was left out. What happened? Why? Compare this model to real rocks, weathering, and erosion. How are they alike? How are they different?

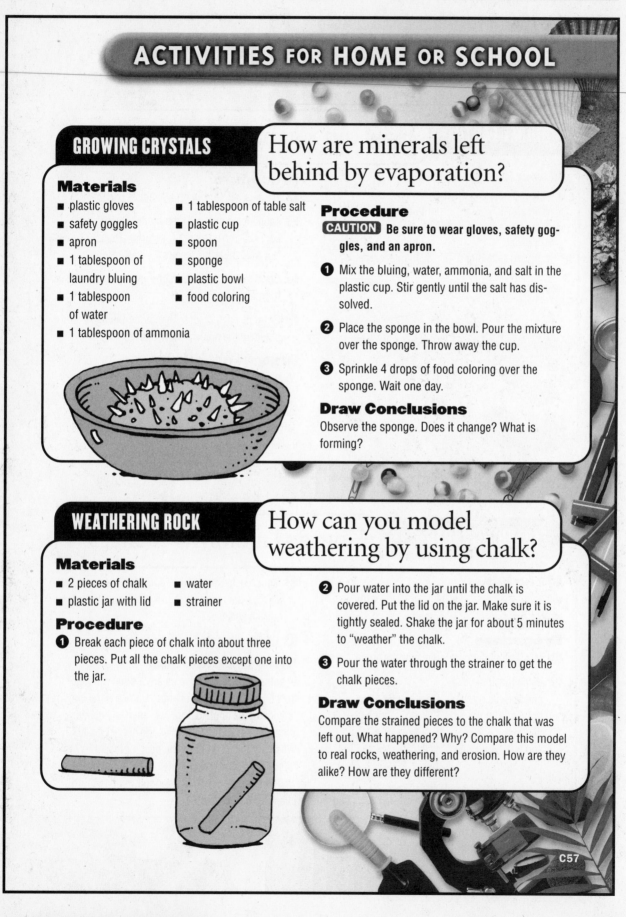

Harcourt

Name _____   Date _____

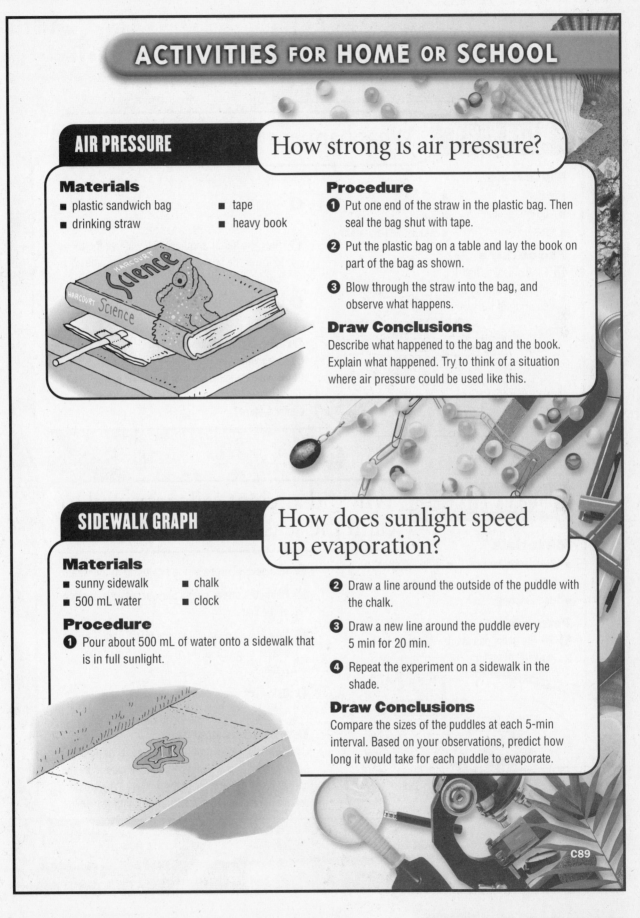

ACTIVITIES FOR HOME OR SCHOOL

AIR PRESSURE

How strong is air pressure?

Materials
- plastic sandwich bag
- drinking straw
- tape
- heavy book

Procedure

❶ Put one end of the straw in the plastic bag. Then seal the bag shut with tape.

❷ Put the plastic bag on a table and lay the book on part of the bag as shown.

❸ Blow through the straw into the bag, and observe what happens.

Draw Conclusions

Describe what happened to the bag and the book. Explain what happened. Try to think of a situation where air pressure could be used like this.

SIDEWALK GRAPH

How does sunlight speed up evaporation?

Materials
- sunny sidewalk
- 500 mL water
- chalk
- clock

Procedure

❶ Pour about 500 mL of water onto a sidewalk that is in full sunlight.

❷ Draw a line around the outside of the puddle with the chalk.

❸ Draw a new line around the puddle every 5 min for 20 min.

❹ Repeat the experiment on a sidewalk in the shade.

Draw Conclusions

Compare the sizes of the puddles at each 5-min interval. Based on your observations, predict how long it would take for each puddle to evaporate.

C89

Harcourt

Name _____ Date _____

ACTIVITIES FOR HOME OR SCHOOL

WATER WORLD

What happens when waters meet?

Materials

- water
- 200-mL beaker
- food coloring
- hot plate
- tongs
- water-filled aquarium

Procedure

❶ Fill the beaker half-full of water. Add food coloring to the water.

❷ Using the hot plate, gently warm the water in the beaker.

❸ Your teacher or another adult will use the tongs to lower the beaker straight down into the aquarium filled with cold water.

❹ Observe the hot, colored water as it leaves the beaker.

Draw Conclusions

Describe what you observed. From your observations, what conclusions can you draw about areas in the ocean where warm currents flow through cooler waters?

OIL AND WATER

Why did ancient sailors use oil to calm the seas near their ships?

Materials

- glass bread pan
- water
- food coloring
- drinking straw
- cooking oil

Procedure

❶ Fill the glass pan about half-full of water.

❷ Add several drops of food coloring to the water.

❸ Using the straw, gently blow across the surface of the water.

❹ Now slowly pour oil into the water until it forms a layer of oil about 1 cm thick on top of the water.

❺ Using the straw, blow gently across the surface again.

Draw Conclusions

Compare the waves produced in Step 3 with those produced in Step 5. What do you conclude to be the cause of any differences in the waves? Why would sailors pour oil on the water during rough weather?

C125

Harcourt

ACTIVITIES FOR HOME OR SCHOOL

PAPER MOON

How can the moon be used to make a calendar?

Materials
- clock
- 28 white paper plates
- scissors

Procedure
1 Observe the moon at the same time each night for 4 weeks.

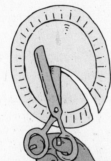

2 Cut one paper plate each night to represent the shape of the moon as you observed it.

3 Hang the paper-plate moons on a wall to make a record of your observations.

Draw Conclusions
How did the shape of the moon change over the length of your observations? What pattern do you notice about the changing shape of the moon? An Earth calendar has 12 months. How many months (moon cycles) would there be in a moon calendar?

SOLAR-SYSTEM DISTANCES

How far is it to Pluto?

Materials
- table of planets' distances from the sun
- roll of toilet paper
- wood dowel
- marker

Procedure
1 Round off all distances on the table to the nearest million kilometers.

2 Use one square of toilet paper to represent the distance from the sun to Mercury.

3 Divide the distance from the sun to Mercury into all the other distances. The quotient for each problem will be how many toilet-paper squares each planet is from the sun.

4 Put the dowel into the toilet-paper roll. Unroll the paper, count the squares of paper, and label the position for each planet.

Draw Conclusions
How many squares of toilet paper does it take to show the location of Pluto? How much farther from the sun is Pluto than Mercury? Distances in the solar system are huge. The toilet-paper model helps you visualize those distances. What kind of model could you make to show the sizes of the planets?

D31

Harcourt

Name _____ Date _____

ACTIVITIES FOR HOME OR SCHOOL

A MODEL SUN

What are some sun features?

Materials
- yellow construction paper
- ruler
- scissors
- markers
- black construction paper
- glue
- white legal-sized paper

Procedure

❶ Cut a 20-cm circle from the yellow paper to represent the photosphere. Using markers, make sunspots on the photosphere.

❷ Cut a 20-cm circle from the black paper to represent the moon during a solar eclipse.

❸ Glue the yellow circle to the white paper.

❹ Using the markers, color jagged shapes around the sun to represent the sun's corona.

❺ Use your black "moon" to eclipse the sun's photosphere to study its corona.

Draw Conclusions

Why did you cut out the moon for the total eclipse the same size as the sun? Scientists learn a great deal about the sun during total eclipses. Why is this an important time to study the sun? What benefits are there to blocking out the sun's photosphere?

ASTROLABE

How do people navigate by the stars?

Materials
- 15-cm cardboard square
- protractor
- pencil
- drinking straw
- tape
- 20-cm piece of string
- metal washer

Procedure

❶ Using the protractor, and starting in one corner of the cardboard square, draw a line at an angle of 5°. Draw additional lines at 10°, 15°, and so on.

❷ Tape the straw to the cardboard as shown.

❸ At the point where all the lines meet, make a hole in the cardboard. Push the string through the hole and tie a knot to keep it from pulling through the hole. Tie the washer to the other end of the string.

❹ Look at the North Star through the straw. Measure the angle of the North Star by noting the angle of the string.

Draw Conclusions

The angle of the North Star tells you your latitude on the Earth. What is the angle of the North Star where you live? What is the latitude where you live?

Harcourt

Use with page D61.

D61

Name _____ Date _____

ACTIVITIES for HOME or SCHOOL

DENSITY COLUMN

Why do some liquids separate?

Materials

- 250-mL graduate
- 50 mL cooking oil
- 50 mL water
- blue food coloring
- 50 mL corn syrup
- 50 mL alcohol
- small cork
- glass marble
- small rock
- wood cube
- metal nut

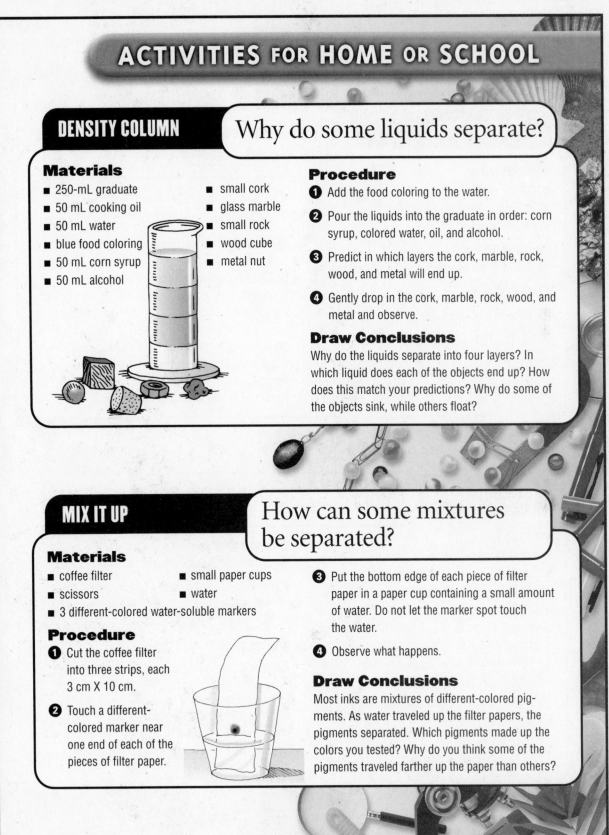

Procedure

1. Add the food coloring to the water.
2. Pour the liquids into the graduate in order: corn syrup, colored water, oil, and alcohol.
3. Predict in which layers the cork, marble, rock, wood, and metal will end up.
4. Gently drop in the cork, marble, rock, wood, and metal and observe.

Draw Conclusions

Why do the liquids separate into four layers? In which liquid does each of the objects end up? How does this match your predictions? Why do some of the objects sink, while others float?

MIX IT UP

How can some mixtures be separated?

Materials

- coffee filter
- scissors
- 3 different-colored water-soluble markers
- small paper cups
- water

Procedure

1. Cut the coffee filter into three strips, each 3 cm X 10 cm.
2. Touch a different-colored marker near one end of each of the pieces of filter paper.
3. Put the bottom edge of each piece of filter paper in a paper cup containing a small amount of water. Do not let the marker spot touch the water.
4. Observe what happens.

Draw Conclusions

Most inks are mixtures of different-colored pigments. As water traveled up the filter papers, the pigments separated. Which pigments made up the colors you tested? Why do you think some of the pigments traveled farther up the paper than others?

Harcourt

E31

Name _____   Date _____

ACTIVITIES FOR HOME OR SCHOOL

ESCAPING GAS

How can you release dissolved gas?

Materials
- 250-mL beaker
- 200 mL carbonated soft drink
- 1 teaspoon sugar

Procedure
1. Pour the carbonated drink into the beaker.
2. Add the sugar.
3. Observe what happens.
4. Repeat the procedure with different brands of soft drinks.

Draw Conclusions

Carbonated soft drinks contain flavorings, colorings, water, and dissolved carbon dioxide gas. You probably heard some of the gas escape when you opened the can or bottle the soft drink came in. The remainder of the carbon dioxide comes out of the soft drink slowly over time. What happened when you added sugar to the drink? What do you think the foam is made of? Did different carbonated drinks behave differently when the sugar was added? Explain.

PERIODIC TABLE

Where are various elements found?

Materials
- a copy of the periodic table
- poster board
- tape
- string
- various objects, such as a helium-filled balloon, a piece of charcoal, an aluminum can, a glass bottle, garden fertilizer, an eggshell, a steel nail, an old penny, a fishing weight

Procedure
1. Mount the periodic table on the poster board.
2. Tape one end of a piece of string to the balloon, and the other end to *He* (helium) on the periodic table.
3. Tape string to all the objects.
4. Tape the other end of each string to the correct element on the periodic table.

Draw Conclusions

Which elements are found in these common objects? Why can't you find objects for all the elements on the periodic table?

Elements in Our Daily Lives

Harcourt

Use with page E53.

E53

ACTIVITIES FOR HOME OR SCHOOL

MAKING MAGNETS

How does an object become a magnet?

Materials
- compass
- sewing needle
- small piece of thin Styrofoam
- shallow bowl of water
- bar magnet

Procedure
❶ Put the compass on the table. Observe the direction the north-seeking end points to.

❷ Put the needle on the piece of Styrofoam, and float it in the bowl of water. Observe which way the needle points.

❸ Now stroke the needle with the bar magnet.

❹ Put the needle back on the floating Styrofoam. Which way does the needle point?

Draw Conclusions
Does the needle act like a compass in Step 2? Does it act like a compass in Step 4? How did you turn the needle into a magnet?

CENTER OF GRAVITY

How can you find an object's center of gravity?

Materials
- 10-cm square of paper
- flat toothpick
- 30 cm of 24-gauge wire
- cardboard cutout of your state

Procedure
❶ Fold the paper in half, and then in half again. Balance the paper on your finger.

❷ Balance the toothpick on your finger.

❸ Straighten out the wire. Then fold the wire in half. Wrap the midpoint of the wire tightly around the toothpick. Now balance the toothpick on your finger.

❹ Using the cardboard cutout and what you have learned about balancing objects, find the geographic center of your state.

Draw Conclusions
An object's center of gravity is the point at which the force of gravity is evenly balanced. Where is the center of gravity of the toothpick? When you added weight (the wire) to the toothpick, what happened to its center of gravity? How did the cardboard cutout's center of gravity help you find the geographic center of your state?

F27

Harcourt

ACTIVITIES FOR HOME OR SCHOOL

IT'S THE LAW

How does a rocket demonstrate the third law of motion?

Materials
- 5 m of string
- drinking straw
- rubber balloon
- double-backed tape

Procedure
❶ Thread the string through the straw. Then hold the ends of the string or tie them to stationary objects.

❷ Blow up the balloon and pinch the end.

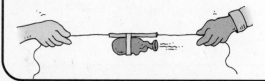

❸ While you hold the balloon, have a partner tape the balloon to the straw.

❹ When the balloon is taped to the straw, release the balloon. Observe the balloon.

Draw Conclusions
What is the third law of motion? What is the action force in your balloon rocket? What is the reaction force? Do you think the action force and the reaction force are equal? In what direction did the air push out? How could you make a more powerful balloon rocket?

SPIN FACTOR

What forces act on a spinning object?

Materials
- fishing weight
- string
- paper-towel tube
- rubber band

Procedure
CAUTION Do this activity in an open area, away from buildings and other people.

❶ Tie the weight to one end of the string. Tie the rubber band to the other end of the string. Then thread the weight through the paper-towel tube.

❷ Holding the paper-towel tube with one hand and the rubber band with your other hand, carefully spin the weight in a circle over your head. Observe the rubber band.

❸ As you spin the weight, slowly pull the string through the tube. Try to keep the weight spinning at the same rate.

❹ Observe what happens to the stretch of the rubber band.

Draw Conclusions
The variables you are experimenting with are the momentum, velocity, and mass of the weight and the radius of the weight's orbit. When you pulled the string through the tube, which variable changed? How did changing that variable change the forces acting on the weight?

F55

Harcourt

Name _____ Date _____

SOUND WAVES

How do sound waves travel?

Materials

- glass pie pan with 200 mL water
- overhead projector
- tuning fork
- balloon
- tin can
- uncooked rice
- Slinky

Procedure

1. Put the pie pan with water on the projector. Turn the projector on.

2. Tap the tuning fork on a solid object. Place the end of the fork in the water. Observe the waves on the screen.

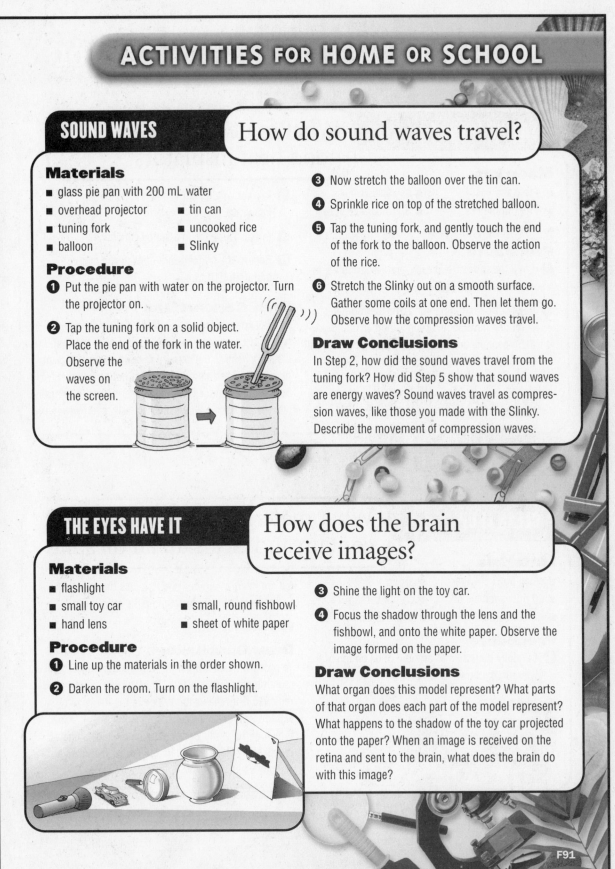

3. Now stretch the balloon over the tin can.

4. Sprinkle rice on top of the stretched balloon.

5. Tap the tuning fork, and gently touch the end of the fork to the balloon. Observe the action of the rice.

6. Stretch the Slinky out on a smooth surface. Gather some coils at one end. Then let them go. Observe how the compression waves travel.

Draw Conclusions

In Step 2, how did the sound waves travel from the tuning fork? How did Step 5 show that sound waves are energy waves? Sound waves travel as compression waves, like those you made with the Slinky. Describe the movement of compression waves.

THE EYES HAVE IT

How does the brain receive images?

Materials

- flashlight
- small toy car
- hand lens
- small, round fishbowl
- sheet of white paper

Procedure

1. Line up the materials in the order shown.

2. Darken the room. Turn on the flashlight.

3. Shine the light on the toy car.

4. Focus the shadow through the lens and the fishbowl, and onto the white paper. Observe the image formed on the paper.

Draw Conclusions

What organ does this model represent? What parts of that organ does each part of the model represent? What happens to the shadow of the toy car projected onto the paper? When an image is received on the retina and sent to the brain, what does the brain do with this image?

F91

Name _____ Date _____

ACTIVITIES FOR HOME OR SCHOOL

SAVING ENERGY

What materials make good heat insulators?

Materials
- 4 tin cans
- 4 thermometers
- cotton batting
- newspaper
- Styrofoam peanuts

Procedure
❶ Put a thermometer in each can. Record the temperature of each can.

❷ Pack cotton batting around one thermometer, shredded newspaper around another, and Styrofoam peanuts around a third. The control can will have a thermometer only.

❸ Predict which item will be the best heat insulator.

❹ Put all four cans in a sunny window.

❺ Record the temperature of each can every minute for 10 min.

Draw Conclusions
In this experiment you tested three items that could help conserve energy. Which material was the best insulator? Home builders try to build energy-efficient homes. Design an energy-efficient house for an outdoor pet. Remember that the house may need to protect the pet from cold weather as well as hot weather.

CLEAN IT UP

What materials can be used to contain and clean up an oil spill?

Materials
- small bowl of water
- 20 mL vegetable oil
- rubber bands
- string
- cotton batting
- paper towels

Procedure
❶ Carefully pour a small amount of oil on top of the water in the bowl.

❷ Brainstorm different ways to use the materials to contain the spill or clean up the oil.

❸ Try out your ideas.

Draw Conclusions
To protect the environment from damage, an oil spill must be contained quickly. Then the oil must be removed from the water. Which of the items you tested were most helpful in containing the oil spill? Which of the items were most helpful in cleaning up the oil spill? Research to find out what materials are actually used.

F117

Harcourt

Vocabulary Activities

The word cards on pages 93–156 contain all the glossary words for Grade 5. The activities listed here suggest ways to use the word cards to do the following:

- increase students' understanding of science terms and concepts.
- help students develop their decoding and encoding (word identification and spelling) skills.
- meet the individual needs of your classroom.

Concept Activities

1. Analogies

Grouping: Whole class or large group (Easy); small group or pairs (Average and Challenge)

Materials: word cards, chalk; paper and pencil (Average and Challenge)

Explain that in an analogy two pairs of words are related to each other in the same way. Tell students that to complete an analogy, the words in the second pair must relate to each other in the same way as the words in the first pair. Review some common types of analogies:

- opposites (*hot* is to *cold* as *tall* is to *short*).
- example (*collie* is to *dog* as *rose* is to *flower*).
- part/whole (*toe* is to *foot* as *branch* is to *tree*).
- function (*carpet* is to *floor* as *mitten* is to *hand*).
- process/source (*cooking* is to *heat* as *refrigerating* is to *cold*).

Easy: List the types of analogies as headings in a chart. Then give students the following analogies. Have them discuss how the two sets of words in each analogy are related, and help them decide where the analogy belongs in the chart. (Answers are in parentheses).

- *condensation* is to *evaporation* as *renewable resource* is to *nonrenewable resource* (opposite)

- *individual* is to *population* as *atom* is to *matter* (part/whole)
- *tidal energy* is to *tide* as *solar energy* is to *sun* (process/source)
- *phototropism* is to *tropism* as *acid rain* is to *pollution* (example)
- *cell* is to *tissue* as *tissue* is to *organ* (part/whole)
- *epidermis* is to *palisade layer* as *crust* is to *mantle* (function)

Average: Divide students into small groups or pairs, and have them work together to "solve" incomplete analogies. Use the analogies listed above, omitting the final element. Give students three possible choices to complete each analogy, only one of which is correct. Allow students time to discuss why they chose the words they did.

Challenge: Follow the procedure described in Average, but do not provide students with possible answer choices. Instead, have them look through their glossaries or word cards for a vocabulary word that can complete each analogy. Again, allow students time to discuss their choices.

Harcourt

2. Categories

Grouping: Whole class or large group; pairs (Challenge)

Materials: word cards; paper and pencil (Challenge)

Have students work with words that are clearly related, either looking for words that fit categories, identifying categories, or creating categories. You may wish to use some of the following sets of categories and vocabulary words to begin the activity.

Categories	Vocabulary Words
Layers of Earth	mantle, crust, core
Coal Formation Stages	peat, lignite, anthracite
Ways to Conserve	reduce, recycle, reuse
Parts of a Cell	nucleus, cell membrane, cytoplasm
Kinds of Traits	dominant, recessive, inherited
Parts of a Flower	stamen, pistil, ovary
Forms of Matter	liquid, gas, solid
Phases of the Water Cycle	evaporation, condensation, precipitation

"The words are earthquake, volcano, flood."

"Natural Disasters!"

Easy: Give students the category and help them search through the word cards to find words that fit.

Average: Give students three vocabulary words and have them name a category that describes all three.

Challenge: Have student partners identify their own sets of word cards and categories. Provide time for partners to challenge other pairs to match words and categories. Give them the option of adding a non-vocabulary word to fill out a category.

3. Word Definition Map

Grouping: Whole class or large group; small group (Average); pairs (Challenge)

Materials: words cards, chalk; paper and pencil (Average and Challenge)

Have students explore certain words in depth. Have them use a Word Definition Map to examine a word's definition, its characteristics, and some examples related to the word. On the board, create a map like the one shown below. Go over the format with students, using the vocabulary word *element*.

Harcourt

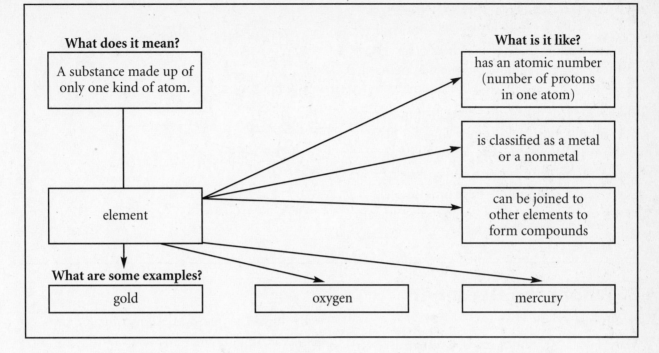

What does it mean?

A substance made up of only one kind of atom.

What is it like?

has an atomic number (number of protons in one atom)

is classified as a metal or a nonmetal

can be joined to other elements to form compounds

element

What are some examples?

gold   oxygen   mercury

Easy: Erase the example word and its related text. Work with students to fill in Word Definitions maps for one or two of these vocabulary words: *angiosperm, galaxy, gas, instinct, liquid, solid, volcano, wetlands.*

Average: Divide students into small groups. List these words on the board: *angiosperm, climate, gas, instinct, liquid, solid, volcano, wetlands.* Have each group choose a word and fill out a Word Definition map. Provide time for students to share their work.

Challenge: Pair students up, and have each pair select one or two vocabulary words to explore, filling out a Word Definition map for each word. Provide time for students to share their completed maps.

4. Password

Grouping: Whole class

Materials: word cards; *Science* glossaries (Easy and Average); timer (Challenge)

Tell students that they will work in teams to guess a "secret" vocabulary word. Explain that one team member will give clues to help the other team member identify a "secret" word. Explain that clue-givers cannot use any form of the word in their clues and that the clues must be brief. You may wish to use a game-show format for the activity by having teams compete against one another. Points can be awarded based on how many clues have been given. For example, 10 points could be given if the word is guessed on the first clue, with fewer points given after each subsequent clue. Point out to teams that they should listen to their opponent's clues as well as their own to help them identify the word.

Easy: Have students work in four-person teams. Explain that on each team, the two guessers and two clue-givers will share responsibilities. Allow students to use the glossary in *Harcourt Science.* Clues may be short phrases (up to 3 words). For additional support, you, as moderator, can identify the part of the alphabet that contains the word ("It's in the A–C portion of the glossary").

Harcourt

Average: Have students work in two-person teams. Challenge students to use one-word clues, and allow them to use the glossary. Have teams keep track of how many clues are needed to guess each "secret" word.

Challenge: Use the format described in Average, but without glossary support. You may also wish to challenge students with a "lightning round": Each team is given 10 vocabulary words and a one-minute time limit to see how close the guesser can come to naming all ten words.

5. What's the Question?

Grouping: Whole class

Materials: 3 × 5 index cards and pencils, *Science* glossaries, chalk; three clickers (Average and Challenge)

Point out to students that most often a question is asked and then an answer is given. Explain that in this activity, they will reverse the process. Tell them that they will be given an answer that is the meaning of a vocabulary word. For each answer, they must tell the word that is defined, in the form of a question. For example if the answer is "It's the state of matter that has no definite shape or volume," the question would be "What is a gas?" Give each student an index card and ask them to write one answer followed by the related question. You may wish to provide students with the following frames:

(Answer) It's a word that means _____.

(Question) What does _____ mean?

Easy: Have students work in groups of four, with one student acting as moderator by reading aloud an answer. Tell the remaining three students that they can use their word cards and glossaries to help them write down the question. Allow time for students to compare their answers.

Average: Follow the procedure described in Easy, but have the three students compete to be the first to give the question aloud. Have students give themselves points for each correct question.

Challenge: Have each student write 6 answers and questions, using 1 vocabulary word per unit. Tell them to write the unit title on the back of the card. Collect the cards for each unit and place them face down. Have students choose a card from each unit in sequence. Award points for each correct question.

6. Jumbles

Grouping: Whole class (Easy); pairs (Average and Challenge)

Materials: word cards, chalk, paper and pencil

Guide students to scramble the letters of vocabulary words, and give hints for unscrambling them. Provide an example such as the following to help students understand the format:

Easy: Work with the whole class, jumbling shorter vocabulary words such as *cell* or *speed*, and using the glossary entries as clues.

Average: Have students work in pairs, swapping jumbles.

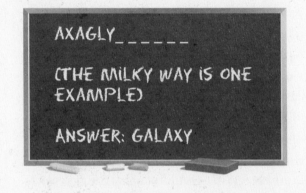

Challenge: Have students choose a short vocabulary word to be their "hidden" word. Then have them find two or three words that share the hidden word's letters. Tell students to create jumbles for the words they find and number the dashes consecutively. Finally, tell them to write a clue for the hidden word, providing appropriately numbered dashes. Have them exchange jumbles with another student.

eattor r o t a t e (to turn on an axis)
          1 2 3 4 5 6

merboy e m b r y o (tiny plant inside seed)
          7 8 9 10 11 12

arcoon c o r o n a (sun's atmosphere)
        13 14 15 16 17 18

What's in the center of the earth? c o r e
                                   13 2 1 7

Decoding/Encoding Activities

1. Word Equations

Grouping: Whole class or large group (Easy), small group (Average and Challenge)

Materials: chalk; paper and pencil (Average and Challenge)

Students can use structural analysis to chunk multisyllabic words, creating "equations" that consist of the following:

prefix(es) + root word + suffix = word.

Write the equation on the board and review it with students. To the side, write *Prefixes* and list *com/con-*, *de-*, and *re-*. Then write *Suffixes* and list three entries: *-or/-er*, *-ation/-tion*, and *-ity*. Use *condensation* to model for students how to create an equation (con + dens + ation = condensation).

Easy: Display these word cards: *community, resistor, decomposer, reactivity, receptor, conduction, deposition, reflection, consumer, reclamation, refraction, conductor.* Work on the board with students to "analyze" the words.

Average: Have students work in small groups to find words in their word cards that have one or more of the prefixes listed on the board and one of the suffixes listed. They should then work together to create equations for these words. Provide time for groups to share and compare their work.

Challenge: Students should follow the procedure described in the Average option. They can then work to come up with other words that contain one of the prefixes listed and one of the suffixes listed, creating equations for each word they think of.

---

2. Rhyme Time

Grouping: Whole class (Easy); pairs (Average and Challenge)

Materials: chalk; word cards (Easy); paper and pencil, *Science* glossaries (Average and Challenge)

Students can use vocabulary words to come up with silly phrases that rhyme. Provide some examples such as *tide ride, cyber fiber, and crust rust.*

cyber fiber

Easy: Provide students with several rhyming phrases like those above. Have them choose one phrase to illustrate. Tell them to incorporate the science word's meaning in their illustrations.

Average: Have student pairs brainstorm their own rhyming phrases to illustrate. You may wish to suggest students look through their word cards for one-syllable words that may be easier to rhyme. Have them create illustrations of their silly phrases.

Challenge: Have students create hink-pinks—riddles with rhyming words as answers. For example, "What would you call the gateway to the center of Earth?" (a core door). "What would you call a problem discovered with cells that work together for a specific function?" (a tissue issue).

---

3. Metamorphosis

Grouping: Whole class (Easy); pairs (Average); small groups (Challenge)

Materials: chalk, drawing materials, word cards (Easy); word cards or *Science* glossaries, paper and pencil, drawing materials (Average and Challenge)

Remind students that metamorphosis is a change in the shape or characteristics of an organism's body. Explain to students that they can change "caterpillar" words into "butterfly" words.

Easy: Pull out some of the shorter vocabulary word cards (e.g., *core, mass, tide, cell, shore, heat, lens*). For each word, guide students to write as many new words as they can by changing one letter. For example, *core* might yield *care, cure, bore, more, sore, tore, wore, code, come, cone, cope, cove, cork,* and *corn.* Students can pick one pair to illustrate (see Average option).

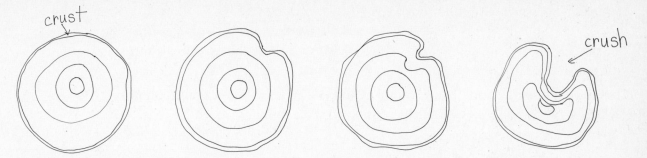

crust

crush

Average: Have student pairs change 3–4 words. Ask them to pick one pair to illustrate, showing how the illustration for the vocabulary word "morphs" into the illustration for the new word.

Challenge: Have teams come up with word chains, transforming a vocabulary word, one letter at a time, into a very different word of the same length. Demonstrate on the board, showing how each word has only one letter changed in the following chain: _wave, wane, want, went, lent, lens_. Pairs should try to figure out the fewest number of changes needed. (As an extra challenge, the new word can be a vocabulary word too, as in the example on the board.) Pairs can swap chains with other pairs, listing the first and last words only, with dashes used for the other words in the chain.

---

4. Root Relationships

Grouping: Pairs and whole class (Easy and Average); pairs (Challenge)

Materials: chalk, selected word cards; dictionary, paper and pencil (Challenge)

Several vocabulary words contain common roots that students can explore.

Easy: Put the following roots/combining forms and meanings on the board as headings for columns: _bio_ ("life"); _ced/cess_ ("to go or yield"); _duc/duct_ ("to lead"); _photo_ ("light"). Have pairs of students collect these word cards: _biomass, biome, conduction, conductor, photosphere, photosynthesis, phototropism, producer, recessive trait, reduce, succession,_ and _symbiosis._ Ask them to shuffle the cards together and then sort them into columns of words that share one of the word parts listed on the board. When students are done, work together to list the words they have identified for each column on the board. Ask volunteers to underline the shared roots/combining forms.

Average: Follow the procedure described in the Easy option. Then have students add other words to each list (_e.g., biology, biography, process, precede, introduce, education, photograph, telephoto lens_). End by discussing how the meaning of the words with bio and photo are related to the meaning of the combining forms they contain.

In phototropism, a plant turns toward light.

Challenge: Use the word cards listed in Easy, supplementing them with _condensation, density, deposition, diffusion, fusion energy,_ and _position._ Have student pairs sort the 18 words by shared root or combining form and then use a dictionary to look up the meaning of each root or combining form. Ask them to choose one group of words to explore further, discussing how the meaning of the root or combining form influences word meaning. Have them think of other words that contain the same word part. Give students a chance to share and compare their work.

Harcourt

Vocabulary Activities

Vocabulary Cards

cell	diffusion
cell membrane	osmosis
nucleus	tissue
cytoplasm	organ

Harcourt

[di·fyoo′zhən]
The process by which many materials move in and out of cells (A10)

[sel]
The basic unit of structure and function of all living things (A6)

[os·mō′sis]
The diffusion of water and dissolved materials through cell membranes (A10)

[sel′ mem′brān′]
The thin covering that encloses a cell and holds its parts together (A8)

[tish′oo]
Cells that work together to perform a specific function (A12)

[noo′klē·əs]
1 *(cell)* The organelle that controls all of a cell's activities. 2 *(atom)* The center of an atom. (A8, E39)

[ôr′gən]
Tissues that work together to perform a specific function (A12)

[sīt′ō·plaz′əm]
A jellylike substance containing many chemicals that keep a cell functioning (A9)

system	nephrons
capillaries	bone marrow
alveoli	joint
villi	tendons

Harcourt

[nef´ronz´] **Tubes inside the kidneys where urea and water diffuse from the blood (A20)**	[sis´təm] **Organs that work together to perform a function (A12)**
[bōn´ mar´ō] **A connective tissue that produces red and white blood cells (A24)**	[kap´ə·ler´ēz] **The smallest blood vessels (A17)**
[joint] **A place where bones meet and are attached to each other and to muscles (A24)**	[al·vē´ə·li] **Tiny air sacs located at the ends of bronchi in the lungs (A18)**
[ten´dənz] **Tough bands of connective tissue that attach muscles to bones (A25)**	[vil´ī] **The tiny tubes sticking into the small intestine (A19)**

Harcourt

ligament	kingdom
neuron	moneran
receptors	protist
classification	fungi

Harcourt

[king′dəm]
The largest group into which living things can be classified (A39)

[lig′ə·mənt]
One of the bands of connective tissue that hold a skeleton together (A25)

[mō·ner′ən]
The kingdom of classification for organisms that have only one cell and no nucleus (A39)

[no͞or′on]
A specialized cell that can receive information and transmit it to other cells (A26)

[prō′tist]
The kingdom of classification for organisms that have only one cell and also have a nucleus, or cell control center (A39)

[ri·sep′tərz]
Nerve cells that detect conditions in the body's environment (A26)

[fun′jī]
Living things that look like plants but cannot make their own food; examples, mushrooms (A39)

[klas′ə·fə·kā′shən]
The grouping of things by using a set of rules (A38)

Harcourt

genus	reptiles
species	amphibians
vertebrates	fish
mammals	birds

[rep´tīlz] **Animals that have dry, scaly skin (A44)**	[jə´nəs] **The second-smallest name grouping used in classification (A40)**
[am·fib´ē·ənz] **Animals that have moist skin and no scales (A44)**	[spē´shēz] **The smallest name grouping used in classification (A40)**
[fish] **Vertebrates that live their entire life in water (A44)**	[vûr´tə·brits] **Animals with a backbone (A44)**
[bûrdz] **Vertebrates with feathers (A45)**	[mam´əlz] **Animals that have hair and produce milk for their young (A44)**

Harcourt

invertebrates	mitosis
vascular plants	asexual reproduction
nonvascular plants	sexual reproduction
chromosome	meiosis

Harcourt

[mī·tō′sis]
The process of cell division (A65)

[in·vûr′tə·brits]
Animals without a backbone (A45)

[ā·sek′shoo·əl rē′prə·duk′shən]
Reproduction by simple cell division (A67)

[vas′kyə·lər plants′]
Plants that have tubes (A50)

[sek′shoo·əl rē′prə·duk′shən]
The form of reproduction in which cells from two parents unite to form a zygote (A68)

[non·vas′kyə·lər plants′]
The plants that do not have tubes (A52)

[mī·ō′sis]
The process that reduces the number of chromosomes in reproductive cells (A68)

[krō′mə·sōm′]
A threadlike strand of DNA inside the nucleus (A65)

Harcourt

life cycle	dominant trait
direct development	recessive trait
metamorphosis	gene
inherited trait	xylem

Harcourt

[dom′ə·nənt trāt′] **A strong trait (A79)**	[līf′ sī·kəl] **All the stages of an organism's life (A72)**
[ri·ses′iv trāt′] **A weak trait (A79)**	[də·rekt′ di·vel′əp·mənt] **A kind of growth where organisms keep the same body features as they grow larger (A72)**
[jēn] **Structure on chromosomes that contains the DNA codes for a trait an organism inherits (A80)**	[met′ə·môr′fə·sis] **A change in the shape or characteristics of an organism's body as it grows (A73)**
[zī′ləm] **The tubes that transport water and minerals in vascular plants (A97)**	[in·her′it·əd trāt′] **A characteristic that is passed from parent to offspring (A78)**

Harcourt

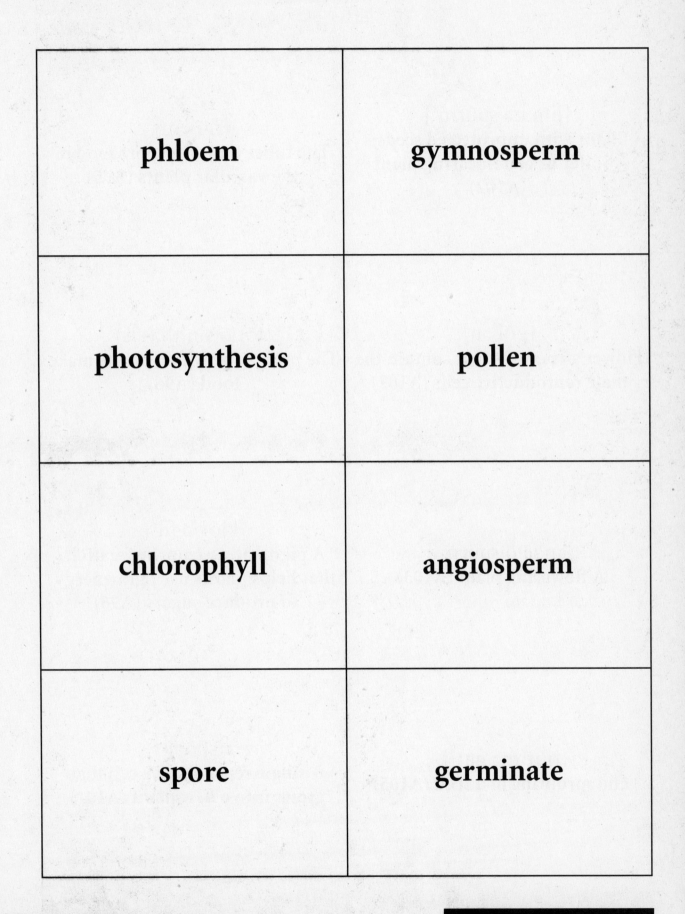

phloem	gymnosperm
photosynthesis	pollen
chlorophyll	angiosperm
spore	germinate

Harcourt

[jim′nə·spûrm′]
Plant with unprotected seeds; conifer or cone-bearing plant (A102)

[flō′em]
The tubes that transport food in the vascular plants (A95)

[pol′ən]
Flower structures that contain the male reproductive cells (A102)

[fōt′ō·sin′thə·sis]
The process by which plants make food (A96)

[an′jē·ō·spurm′]
A flowering plant (A103)

[klôr′ə·fil′]
A pigment, or coloring matter, that helps plants use light energy to produce sugars (A96)

[jûr′mə·nāt′]
The sprouting of a seed (A105)

[spôr]
A single reproductive cell that grows into a new plant (A101)

Harcourt

grain	respiration
fiber	water cycle
nitrogen cycle	evaporation
carbon-oxygen cycle	condensation

Harcourt

[res´pə·rā´shən]
The process that releases energy from food (B8)

[grān]
The seed of certain plants (A110)

[wôt´ər sī´kəl]
The cycle in which Earth's water moves through the environment (B14)

[fī´bər]
Any material that can be separated into threads (A112)

[ē·vap´ə·rā´shən]
The process by which a liquid changes into a gas (B14, C67, E16)

[nī´trə·jən sī´kəl]
The cycle in which nitrogen gas is changed into forms of nitrogen that plants can use (B7)

[kon´dən·sā´shən]
The process by which a gas changes back into a liquid (B14, C67, E17)

[kär´bən ok´sə·jən sī´kəl]
The process by which carbon and oxygen cycle among plants, animals, and the environment (B8)

Harcourt

precipitation	community
transpiration	ecosystem
individual	habitat
population	niche

[kə·myo͞o′nə·tē]
All the populations of organisms living together in an environment (B28)

[pri·sip′ə·tā′shən]
Any form of water that falls from clouds, such as rain or snow (B15, C65)

[ēk′ō·sis′təm]
A community and its physical environment together (B28)

[tran′spə·rā′shən]
The process in which plants give off water through their stomata (B15)

[hab′ə·tat′]
A place in an ecosystem where a population lives (B29)

[in′də·vij′o͞o·əl]
A single organism in an environment (B28)

[nich]
The role each population has in its habitat (B29)

[pop·yə·lā′shən]
All the individuals of the same kind living in the same environment (B28)

producer	food web
consumer	energy pyramid
food chain	competition
decomposer	symbiosis

[food′ web′]
**Shows the interactions among
many different food chains in a
single ecosystem (B36)**

[prə·dōōs′ər]
**An organism that makes its own
food (B34)**

[en′ər·jē pir′ə·mid]
**Shows the amount of energy
available to pass from one level of
a food chain to the next (B38)**

[kən·sōō′mər]
**An organism in a community that
must eat to get the energy it needs
(B34)**

[kom′pə·tish′ən]
**The contest among organisms
for the limited resources of
an ecosystem (B42)**

[food′ chān′]
**The ways in which the organisms
in an ecosystem interact with one
another according to what they
eat (B35)**

[sim′bē·ō′sis]
**A long-term relationship between
different kinds of organisms (B45)**

[dē′kəm·pōz′ər]
**Consumer that breaks down the
tissues of dead organisms (B35)**

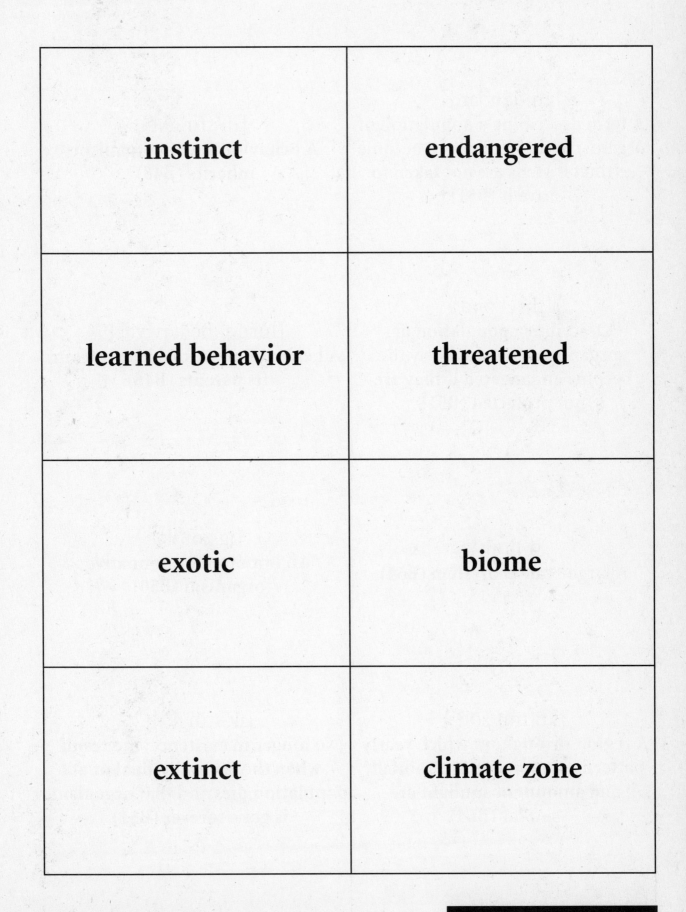

instinct	endangered
learned behavior	threatened
exotic	biome
extinct	climate zone

Harcourt

[en·dān′jərd] **A term describing a population of organisms that is likely to become extinct if steps are not taken to save it (B51)**	[in′stingkt] **A behavior that an organism inherits (B46)**
[thret′ənd] **Describes a population of organisms that are likely to become endangered if they are not protected (B51)**	[lûrnd′ bē·hāv′yər] **A behavior an animal learns from its parents (B46)**
[bī′ōm′] **A large-scale ecosystem (B64)**	[ig·zot′ik] **An imported or nonnative organism (B50)**
[klī′mit zōn′] **A region throughout which yearly patterns of temperature, rainfall, and amount of sunlight are similar (B64)**	[ik·stingkt′] **No longer in existence; the result when the last individual of a population dies and that organism is gone forever (B51)**

Harcourt

intertidal zone	succession
near-shore zone	pioneer plants
open-ocean zone	climax community
estuary	pollution

[sək·sesh′ən]
A gradual change in an ecosystem, sometimes occurring over hundreds of years (B92)

[in′tər·tīd′əl zōn′]
An area where the tide and churning waves provide a constant supply of oxygen and nutrients to living organisms (B77)

[pī′ə·nir′ plants′]
The first plants to invade a bare area (B92)

[nir′shôr′ zōn′]
The area beyond the breaking waves that extends to waters that are about 180 m deep (B77)

[klī′maks′ kə·myoo′nə·tē]
The last stage of succession (B93)

[ō′pən·ō′shən zōn′]
The area that includes most deep ocean waters; most organisms live near the surface (B77)

[pə·loo′shən]
Waste products that damage an ecosystem (B99)

[es′choo·er′ē]
The place where a freshwater river empties into an ocean (B80, C102)

Harcourt

acid rain	recycle
conserving	reclamation
reduce	wetlands
reuse	landform

[rē·sī′kəl]
To recover a resource from an item and use the recovered resource to make a new item (B105)

[as′id rān′]
Precipitation resulting from pollution condensing into clouds and falling to Earth (B99)

[rek′lə·mā′shən]
The process of restoring a damaged ecosystem (B110)

[kən·sûrv′ing]
The saving or protecting of resources (B104)

[wet′landz′]
The water ecosystems that include saltwater marshes, mangrove swamps, and mud flats (B111)

[ri·dōōs′]
To cut down on the use of resources (B104)

[land′fôrm′]
A physical feature on Earth's surface (C6)

[rē′yōōz′]
To use items again, sometimes for a different purpose (B105)

Harcourt

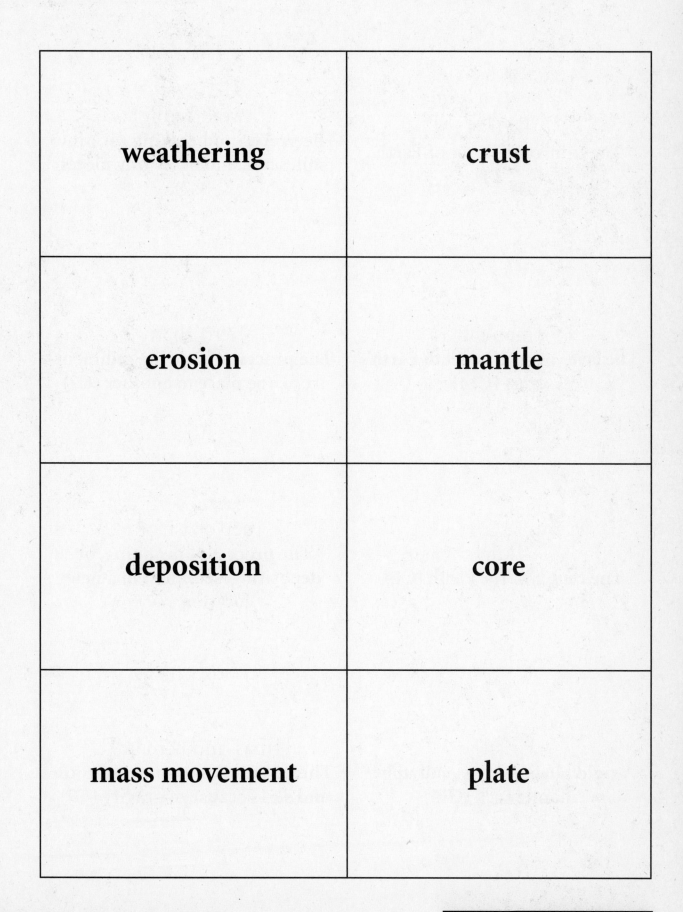

weathering	crust
erosion	mantle
deposition	core
mass movement	plate

Harcourt

[krust] **The thin, outer layer of Earth (C14)**	[weth′ər·ing] **The process of breaking rock into soil, sand, and other tiny pieces (C7)**
[man′təl] **The layer of rock beneath Earth's crust (C14)**	[ē·rō′zhən] **The process of moving sediment from one place to another (C7)**
[kôr] **The center of the Earth (C14)**	[dep′ə·zish′ən] **The process of dropping, or depositing, sediment in a new location (C7)**
[plāt] **A rigid block of crust and upper mantle rock (C15)**	[mas′ moov′mənt] **The downhill movement of rock and soil because of gravity (C9)**

Harcourt

magma	continental drift
volcano	Pangea
earthquake	fossil
fault	mineral

Harcourt

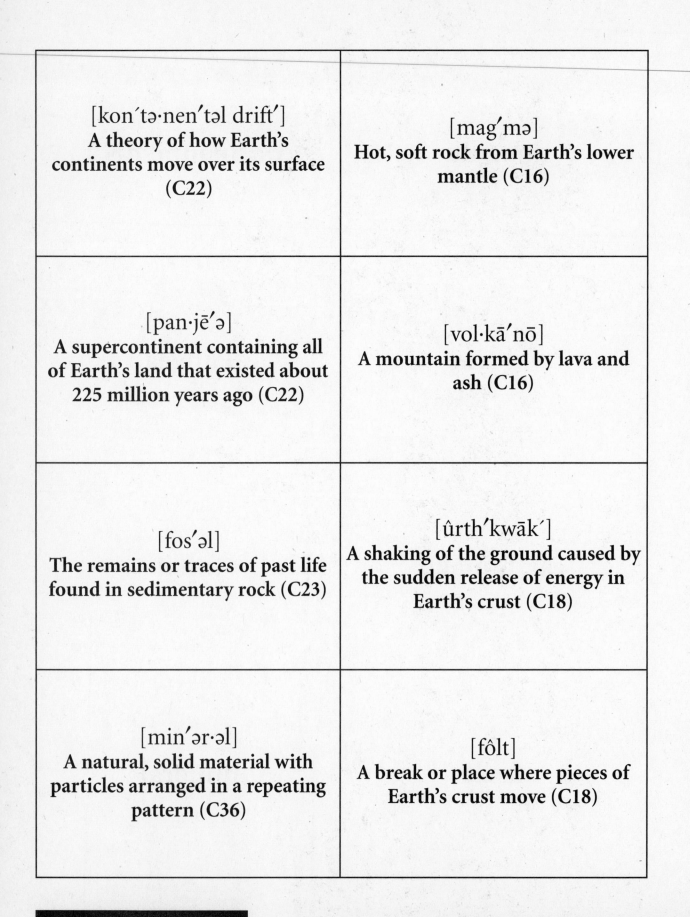

[kon´tə·nen´təl drift´]
A theory of how Earth's continents move over its surface (C22)

[mag´mə]
Hot, soft rock from Earth's lower mantle (C16)

[pan·jē´ə]
A supercontinent containing all of Earth's land that existed about 225 million years ago (C22)

[vol·kā´nō]
A mountain formed by lava and ash (C16)

[fos´əl]
The remains or traces of past life found in sedimentary rock (C23)

[ûrth´kwāk´]
A shaking of the ground caused by the sudden release of energy in Earth's crust (C18)

[min´ər·əl]
A natural, solid material with particles arranged in a repeating pattern (C36)

[fôlt]
A break or place where pieces of Earth's crust move (C18)

Harcourt

streak	igneous rock
luster	sedimentary rock
hardness	metamorphic rock
rock	rock cycle

Harcourt

[igʹnē·əs rokʹ] **A type of rock that forms when melted rock hardens (C42)**	[strēk] **The color of the powder left behind when you rub a material against a white tile called a streak plate (C37)**
[sedʹə·menʹtər·ē rokʹ] **A type of rock formed by layers of sediments that squeezed and stuck together over a long time (C44)**	[lusʹtər] **The way the surface of a mineral reflects light (C37)**
[metʹə·môrʹfik rokʹ] **A type of rock changed by heat or pressure but not completely melted (C46)**	[härdʹnis] **A mineral's ability to resist being scratched (C37)**
[rokʹ sīʹkəl] **The slow, never-ending process of rock changes (C52)**	[rok] **A material made up of one or more minerals (C42)**

Harcourt

atmosphere	evaporation
air pressure	condensation
humidity	local winds
precipitation	prevailing winds

Harcourt

[ē·vap′ə·rā′shən]
The process by which a liquid changes into a gas (B14, C67, E16)

[at′məs·fir]
The layer of air that surrounds Earth (C64)

[kon′dən·sā′shən]
The process by which a gas changes back into a liquid (B14, C67, E17)

[âr′ presh′ər]
The weight of air (C65)

[lō′kəl windz′]
The winds dependent upon local changes in temperature (C73)

[hyoo·mid′ə·tē]
A measure of the amount of water in the air (C65)

[prē·vāl′ing windz′]
The global winds that blow constantly from the same direction (C73)

[pri·sip′ə·tā′shən]
Any form of water that falls from clouds, such as rain or snow (B14, C65)

Harcourt

air mass	El Niño
front	greenhouse effect
climate	global warming
microclimate	salinity

[el′ nēn′yō] **A short-term climate change that occurs every two to ten years in the Pacific Ocean (C83)**	[âr′ mas′] **A large body of air that has nearly the same temperature and humidity throughout (C75)**
[grēn′hous′ i·fekt′] **process by which the Earth's atmosphere absorbs heat (C84)**	[frunt] **The boundary between air masses (C75)**
[glō′bəl wôrm′ing] **The hypothesized rise in Earth's average temperature from excess carbon dioxide (C84)**	[klī′mit] **The average of all weather conditions through all seasons over a period of time (C80)**
[sə·lin′ə·tē] **Saltiness of the ocean (C97)**	[mī′krō·klī′mit] **The climate of a very small area (C80)**

water pressure	shore
wave	headland
current	tide pool
tide	jetty

Harcourt

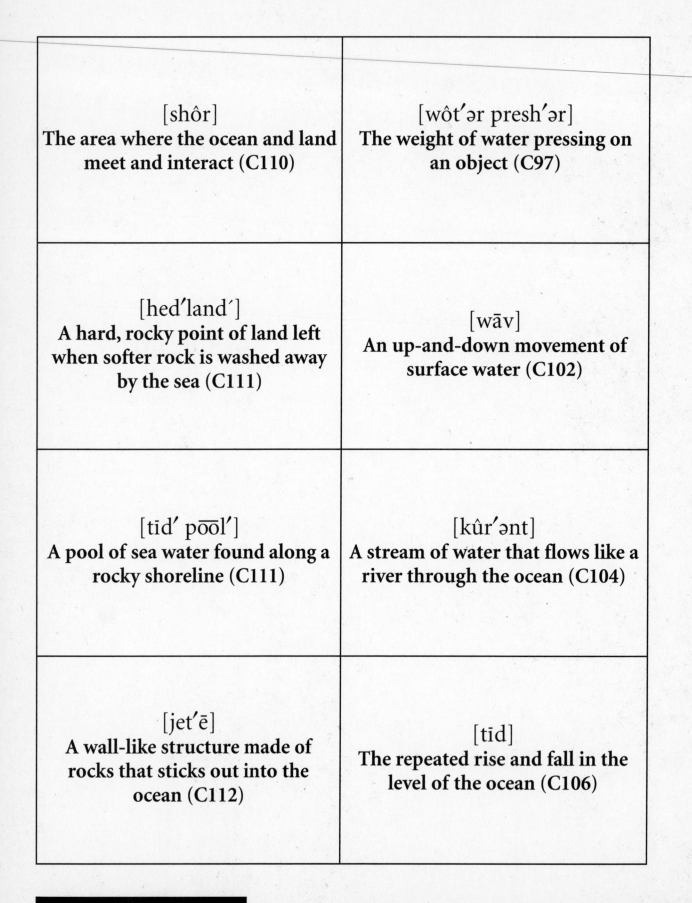

[shôr] The area where the ocean and land meet and interact (C110)	[wôt′ər presh′ər] The weight of water pressing on an object (C97)
[hed′land′] A hard, rocky point of land left when softer rock is washed away by the sea (C111)	[wāv] An up-and-down movement of surface water (C102)
[tīd′ pool′] A pool of sea water found along a rocky shoreline (C111)	[kûr′ənt] A stream of water that flows like a river through the ocean (C104)
[jet′ē] A wall-like structure made of rocks that sticks out into the ocean (C112)	[tīd] The repeated rise and fall in the level of the ocean (C106)

scuba	revolve
submersible	orbit
sonar	rotate
desalination	axis

Harcourt

[ri·volv′] **To travel in a closed path around another object such as Earth does as it moves around the sun (D6)**	[skōō′bə] **Underwater breathing equipment; the letters stand for *s*elf-*c*ontained *u*nderwater *b*reathing *a*pparatus (C117)**
[ôr′bit] **The path one body in space takes as it revolves around another body; such as that of Earth as it revolves around the sun (D7, F48)**	[sub·mûr′sə·bəl] **An underwater vehicle (C117)**
[rō′tāt] **To spin on an axis (D7)**	[sō′när′] **A device that uses sound waves to determine water depth (C117)**
[ak′sis] **An imaginary line that passes through Earth's center and its North and South Poles (D7)**	[dē·sal′ə·nā′shən] **The process of removing salt from sea water (C120)**

Harcourt

eclipse	asteroids
solstice	comets
equinox	telescope
planets	satellite

Harcourt

[as′tə•roidz] **Chunks of rock that look like giant potatoes in space (D16)**	[i•klips′] **The passing of one object through the shadow of another (D8)**
[kom′its] **Balls of ice and rock that circle the sun from two regions beyond the orbit of Pluto (D16)**	[sol′stis] **Point in Earth's orbit at which hours of daylight are at their greatest or fewest (D15)**
[tel′ə•skōp′] **An instrument that magnifies distant objects, or makes them appear larger (D23)**	[ē′kwə•noks′] **Point in Earth's orbit at which the hours of daylight and darkness are equal (D15)**
[sat′ə•līt′] **A natural body, like the moon, or an artificial object that orbits another object (D23)**	[plan′its] **Large, round bodies that revolve around a star (D16)**

space probe	solar flare
photosphere	solar wind
corona	magnitude
sunspot	main sequence

[sō′lər flâr′] **A brief burst of energy from the sun's photosphere (D42)**	[spās′ prōb′] **A robot vehicle used to explore deep space (D24)**
[sō′lər wind′] **A fast-moving stream of particles thrown into space by solar flares (D42)**	[fōt′ə·sfir′] **The visible surface of the sun (D41)**
[mag′nə·tōōd] **Brightness of stars (D46)**	[kə·rō′nə] **The sun's atmosphere (D41)**
[mān′ sē′kwəns] **A band of stars that includes most stars of average color, size, magnitude, and temperature (D47)**	[sun′spot′] **A dark spot on the photosphere of the sun (D42)**

Harcourt

universe	physical properties
galaxy	mass
light-year	weight
matter	volume

Harcourt

[fiz′i·kəl prop′ər·tēz] **The characteristics of a substance that can be observed or measured without changing the substance (E6)**	[yo͞on′ə·vûrs′] **Everything that exists—planets, stars, dust, gases, and energy (D54)**
[mas] **The amount of matter in an object (E7)**	[gal′ək·sē] **A group of stars, with the nearby gas and dust (D54)**
[wāt] **A measure of the pull of gravity on an object (E7)**	[līt′yir′] **The distance light travels in one Earth year; about 9.5 trillion km (D55)**
[vol′yo͞om] **1 *(measurement)* The amount of space that an object takes up. 2 *(sound)* The loudness of a sound (E8, F79)**	[mat′ər] **Anything that has mass and takes up space (E6)**

Harcourt

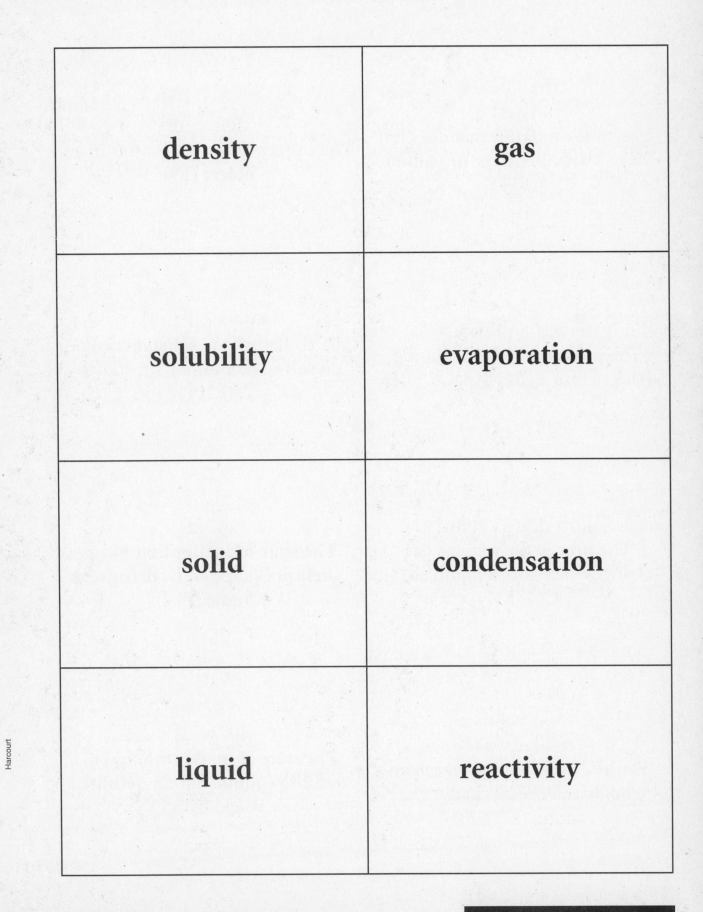

density	gas
solubility	evaporation
solid	condensation
liquid	reactivity

Harcourt

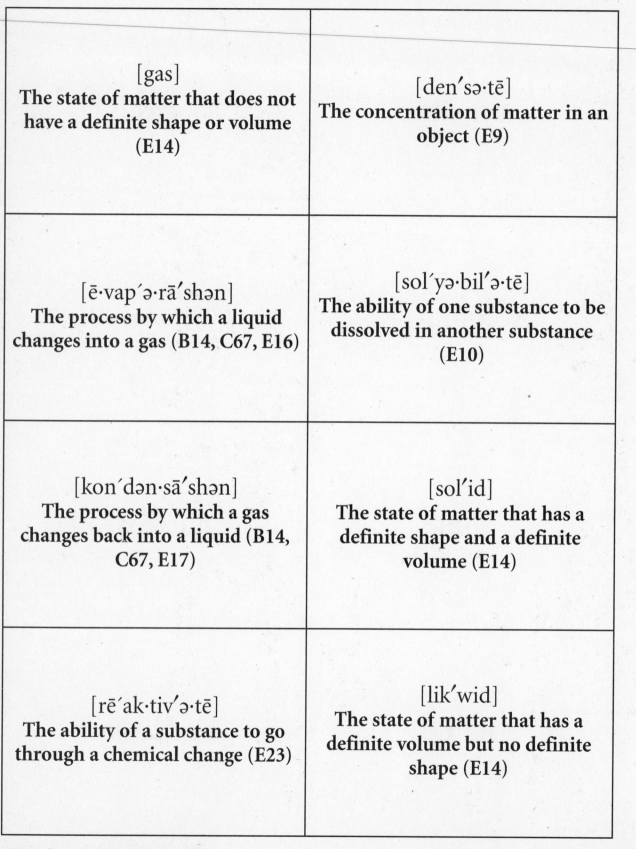

[gas]
The state of matter that does not have a definite shape or volume (E14)

[den′sə·tē]
The concentration of matter in an object (E9)

[ē·vap′ə·rā′shən]
The process by which a liquid changes into a gas (B14, C67, E16)

[sol′yə·bil′ə·tē]
The ability of one substance to be dissolved in another substance (E10)

[kon′dən·sā′shən]
The process by which a gas changes back into a liquid (B14, C67, E17)

[sol′id]
The state of matter that has a definite shape and a definite volume (E14)

[rē′ak·tiv′ə·tē]
The ability of a substance to go through a chemical change (E23)

[lik′wid]
The state of matter that has a definite volume but no definite shape (E14)

Harcourt

combustibility	electron
nucleus	element
proton	atom
neutron	molecule

[ē·lek′tron′]
A subatomic particle with a negative charge (E39)

[kəm·bus′tə·bil′ə·tē]
The chemical property of being able to burn (E24)

[el′ə·mənt]
A substance made up of only one kind of atom (E40)

[nōō′klē·əs]
1 *(cell)* The organelle that controls all of a cell's activities. 2 *(atom)* The center of an atom. (A8, E39)

[at′əm]
The smallest unit of an element that has all the properties of that element (E40)

[prō′ton′]
A subatomic particle with a positive charge (E39)

[mol′ə·kyōōl′]
A grouping of two or more atoms joined together (E40)

[nōō′tron′]
A subatomic particle with no charge (E39)

Harcourt

periodic table	magnetism
compound	gravitation
force	balanced forces
friction	unbalanced forces

[mag′nə·tiz′əm]
**The force of attraction between
magnets and magnetic objects
(F7)**

[pir′ē·od′ik tā′bəl]
**The table of elements in order of
increasing atomic number;
grouped by similar properties
(E47)**

[grav′i·tā′shən]
**The force that pulls all objects in
the universe toward one another
(F8)**

[kom′pound]
**A substance made of the atoms of
two or more different elements
(E48)**

[bal′ənst fôrs′əz]
**The forces acting on an object that
are equal in size and opposite in
direction, canceling each other out
(F12)**

[fôrs]
**A push or pull that causes an
object to move, stop, or change
direction (F6)**

[un·bal′ənst fôrs′əz]
Forces that are not equal (F13)

[frik′shən]
**A force that opposes, or acts
against, motion when two surfaces
rub against each other (F6)**

Harcourt

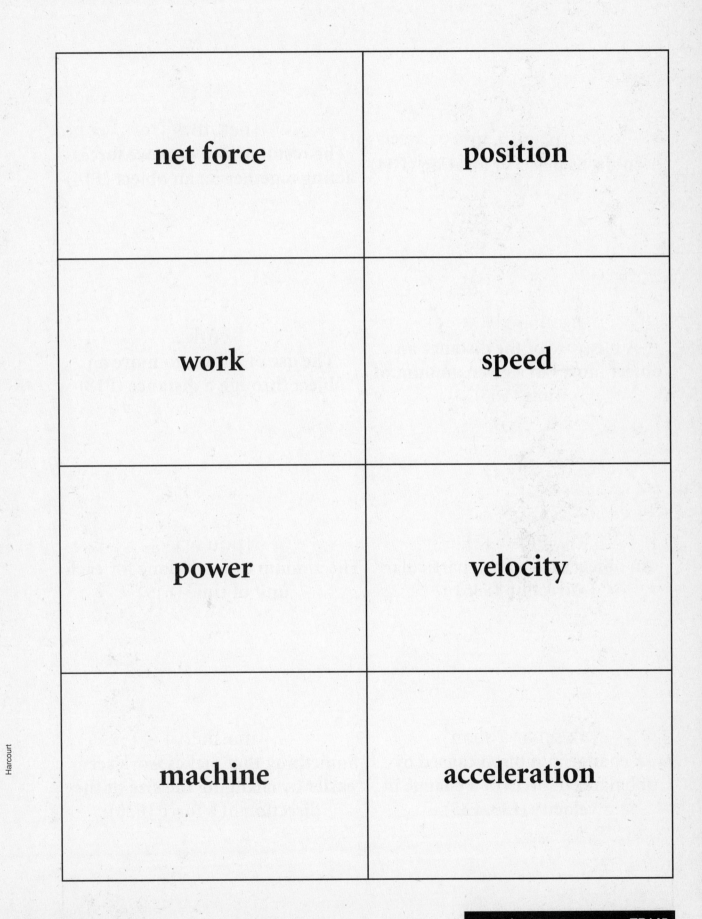

net force	position
work	speed
power	velocity
machine	acceleration

Harcourt

[pə·zish′ən] An object's place, or location (F34)	[net′ fôrs′] The result of two or more forces acting together on an object (F14)
[spēd] A measure of the distance an object moves in a given amount of time (F35)	[wûrk] The use of a force to move an object through a distance (F18)
[və·los′ə·tē] An object's speed in a particular direction (F35)	[pou′ər] The amount of work done for each unit of time (F19)
[ak·sel′ər·ā′shən] A change in motion caused by unbalanced forces or a change in velocity (F13, F35)	[mə·shēn′] Something that makes work seem easier by changing the size or the direction of a force (F20)

Harcourt

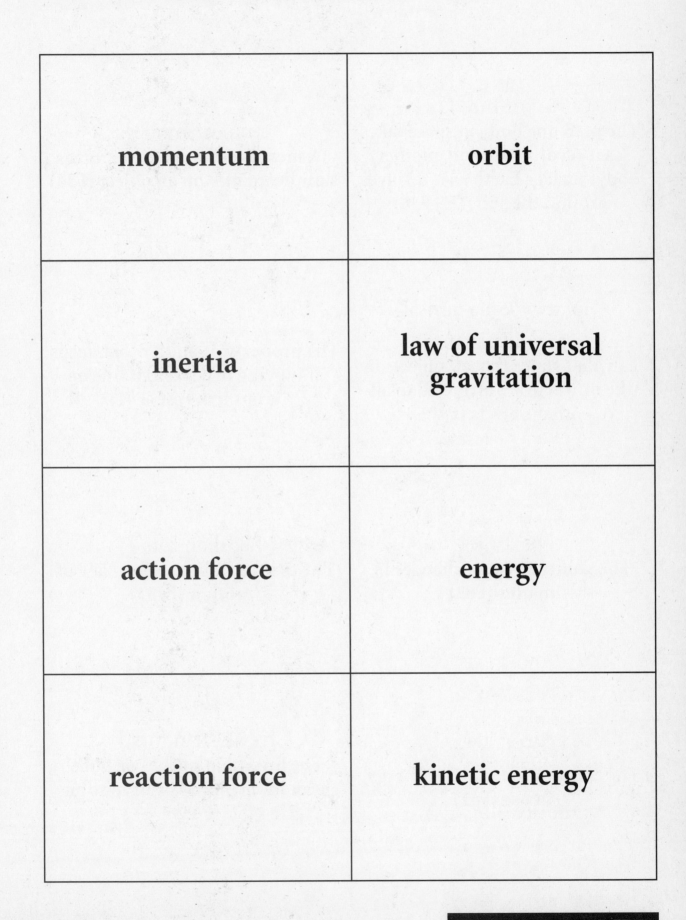

momentum	orbit
inertia	law of universal gravitation
action force	energy
reaction force	kinetic energy

Harcourt

[ôr′bit]
The path one body in space takes as it revolves around another body; such as Earth as it revolves around the sun (D7, F48)

[mō·men′təm]
A measure of how hard it is to slow down or stop an object (F36)

[lô′ uv yōōn′ə·vûr′səl grav′i·tā′shən]
Law that states that all objects in the universe are attracted to all other objects (F49)

[in·ûr′shə]
The property of matter that keeps it moving in a straight line or keeps it at rest (F41)

[en′ər·jē]
The ability to cause changes in matter (F62)

[ak′shən fôrs′]
The first force in the third law of motion (F43)

[ki·net′ik en′ər·jē]
The energy of motion, or energy in use (F62)

[rē·ak′shən fôrs′]
The force that pushes or pulls back in the third law of motion (F43)

potential energy	**conductor**
electric charge	**electric circuit**
electric force	**insulator**
electric current	**resistor**

Harcourt

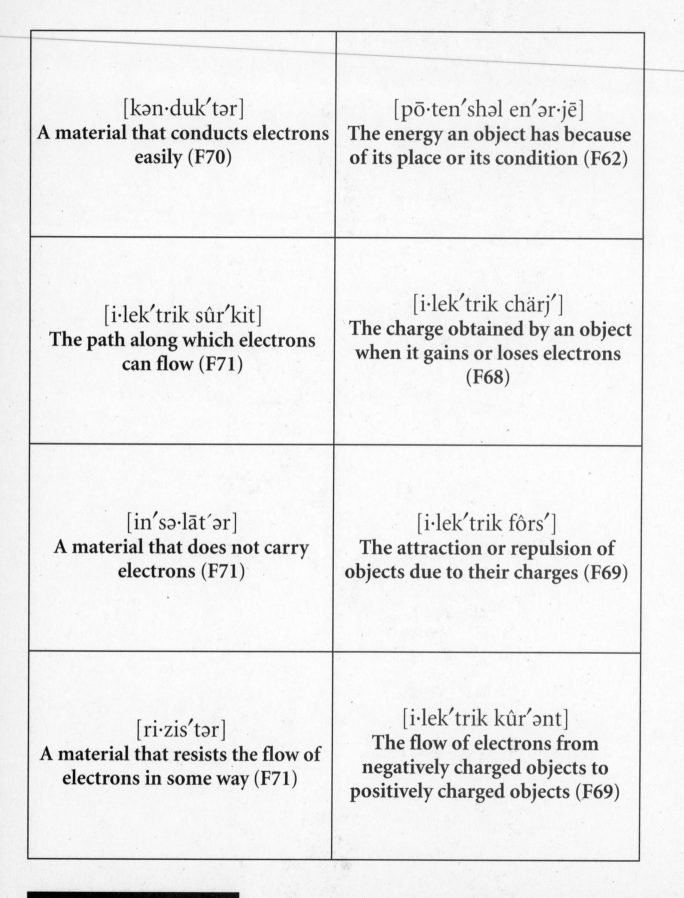

[kən·duk′tər]
A material that conducts electrons easily (F70)

[pō·ten′shəl en′ər·jē]
The energy an object has because of its place or its condition (F62)

[i·lek′trik sûr′kit]
The path along which electrons can flow (F71)

[i·lek′trik chärj′]
The charge obtained by an object when it gains or loses electrons (F68)

[in′sə·lāt′ər]
A material that does not carry electrons (F71)

[i·lek′trik fôrs′]
The attraction or repulsion of objects due to their charges (F69)

[ri·zis′tər]
A material that resists the flow of electrons in some way (F71)

[i·lek′trik kûr′ənt]
The flow of electrons from negatively charged objects to positively charged objects (F69)

Harcourt

electromagnet	pitch
reflection	volume
refraction	temperature
lens	heat

[pich]
An element of sound determined by the speed at which sound waves move (F79)

[i·lek′trō·mag′nit]
A temporary magnet made by passing electric current through a wire coiled around an iron bar (F72)

[vol′yōōm]
1 *(measurement)* The amount of space that an object takes up.
2 *(sound)* The loudness of a sound (E8, F79)

[ri·flek′shən]
The light energy that bounces off objects (F76)

[tem′pər·ə·chər]
The average kinetic energy of all the molecules in an object (F84)

[ri·frak′shən]
The bending of light rays when they pass from one substance to another (F76)

[hēt]
The transfer of thermal energy from one substance to another (F84)

[lenz]
A piece of clear material that bends, or refracts, light rays passing through it (F77)

Harcourt

conduction	hydroelectric energy
convection	tidal energy
radiation	biomass
chemical bonds	nuclear energy

Harcourt

[hī′drō·ē·lek′trik en′ər·jē] **Electricity generated from the force of moving water (F104)**	[kən·duk′shən] **The direct transfer of heat between objects that touch (F85)**
[tīd′əl en′ər·jē] **A form of hydroelectric energy that produces electricity from the rising and falling of tides (F106)**	[kən·vek′shən] **The transfer of heat as a result of the mixing of a liquid or a gas (F85)**
[bī′ō·mas′] **Organic matter, such as wood, that is living or was recently alive (F110)**	[rā′dē·ā′shən] **The transfer of thermal energy by electromagnetic waves (F85)**
[noo′klē·ər en′ər·jē] **The energy released when the nucleus of an atom is split apart (F110)**	[kem′i·kəl bondz′] **The forces that join atoms to each other (F98)**

Harcourt

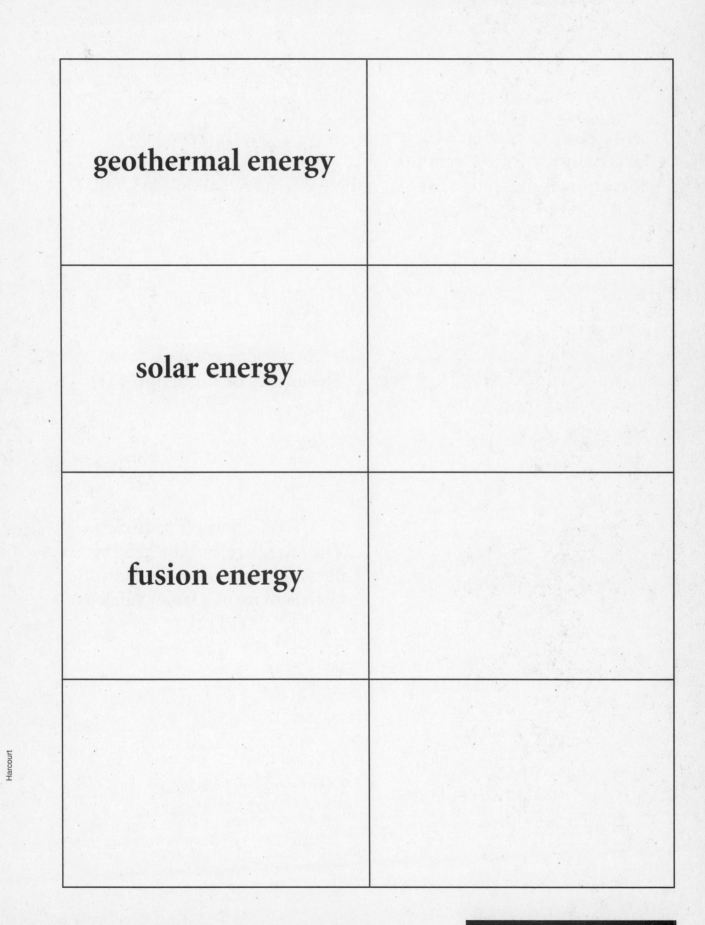

geothermal energy

solar energy

fusion energy

Harcourt

[jē´ō·thûr´məl en´ər·jē]
Heat from inside the Earth (F111)

[sō´lər en´ər·jē]
The energy of sunlight (F111)

[fyoo´zhən en´ər·jē]
**The energy released when the
nuclei of two atoms are forced
together to form a larger nucleus
(F112)**

Harcourt

North American Biomes

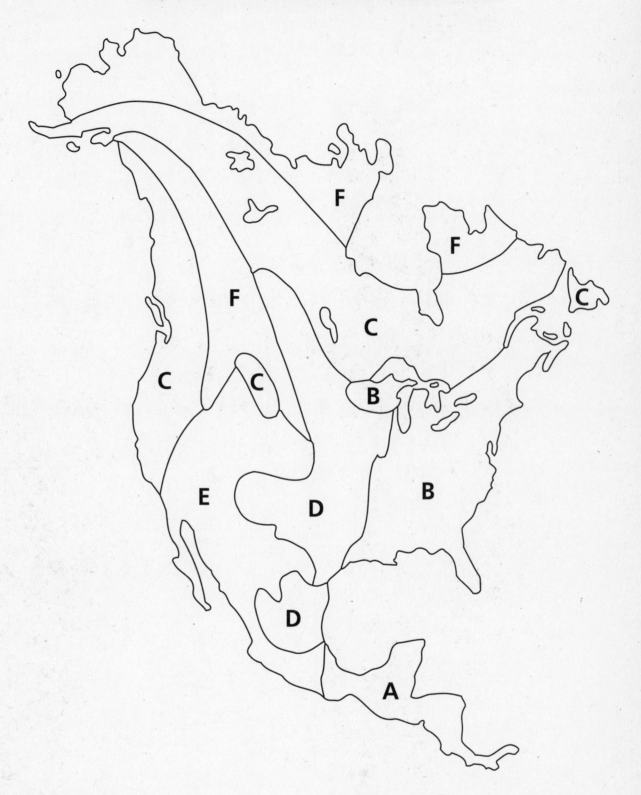

Harcourt

North American Climate Zones

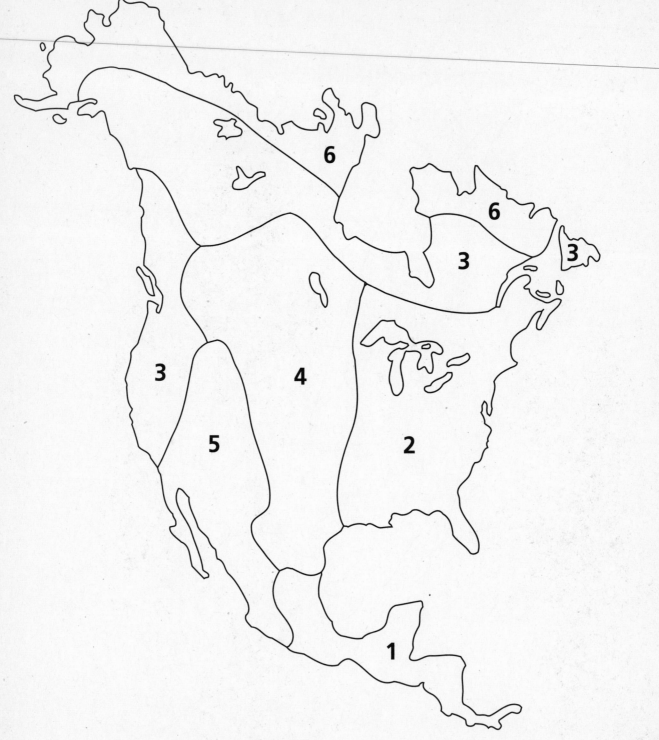

Harcourt

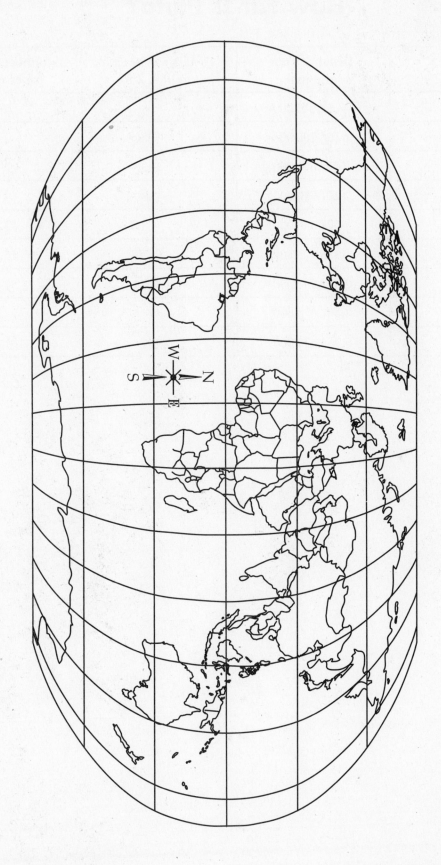

World Map

Distances to Scale
How Far Is Pluto?

Planet	Distance from the Sun	Distance to nearest million km	Number of toilet paper squares
Mercury	57,910,000	58	1
Venus	108,200,000	108	2
Earth	149,600,000	150	2.6
Mars	227,940,000	228	4
Jupiter	778,330,000	778	13.4
Saturn	886,708,500	887	15.2
Uranus	2,870,990,000	2,871	50
Nepture	4,497,070,000	4,497	77.5
Pluto	5,913,520,000	5,914	101

Use with page D31.

Harcourt

Prairie Food Web

The Periodic Table

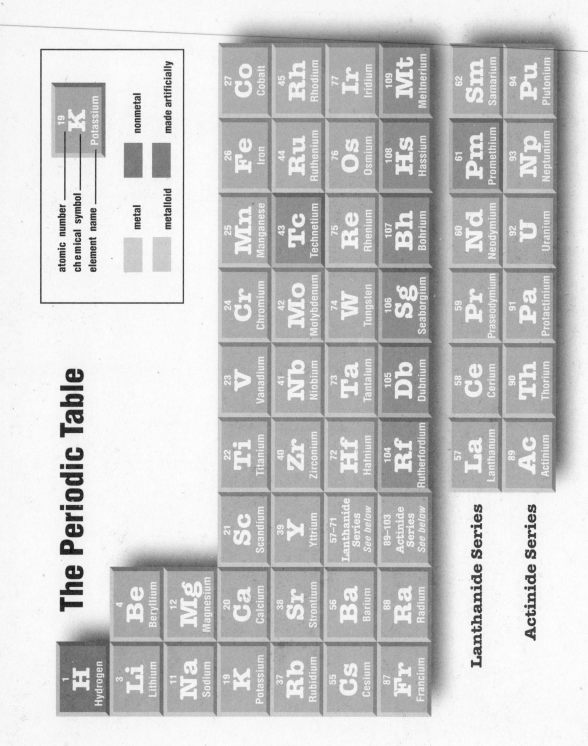

Lanthanide Series

Actinide Series

Harcourt

Am 95 Americium
Cm 96 Curium
Bk 97 Berkelium
Cf 98 Californium
Es 99 Einsteinium
Fm 100 Fermium
Md 101 Mendelevium
No 102 Nobelium
Lr 103 Lawrencium

Eu 63 Europium
Gd 64 Gadolinium
Tb 65 Terbium
Dy 66 Dysprosium
Ho 67 Holmium
Er 68 Erbium
Tm 69 Thulium
Yb 70 Ytterbium
Lu 71 Lutetium

Ni 28 Nickel
Cu 29 Copper
Zn 30 Zinc
Ga 31 Gallium
Ge 32 Germanium
As 33 Arsenic
Se 34 Selenium
Br 35 Bromine
Kr 36 Krypton

Pd 46 Palladium
Ag 47 Silver
Cd 48 Cadmium
In 49 Indium
Sn 50 Tin
Sb 51 Antimony
Te 52 Tellurium
I 53 Iodine
Xe 54 Xenon

Pt 78 Platinum
Au 79 Gold
Hg 80 Mercury
Tl 81 Thallium
Pb 82 Lead
Bi 83 Bismuth
Po 84 Polonium
At 85 Astatine
Rn 86 Radon

B 5 Boron
Al 13 Aluminum
Si 14 Silicon
P 15 Phosphorus
S 16 Sulfur
Cl 17 Chlorine
Ar 18 Argon

C 6 Carbon
N 7 Nitrogen
O 8 Oxygen
F 9 Fluorine
Ne 10 Neon
He 2 Helium

Flowchart

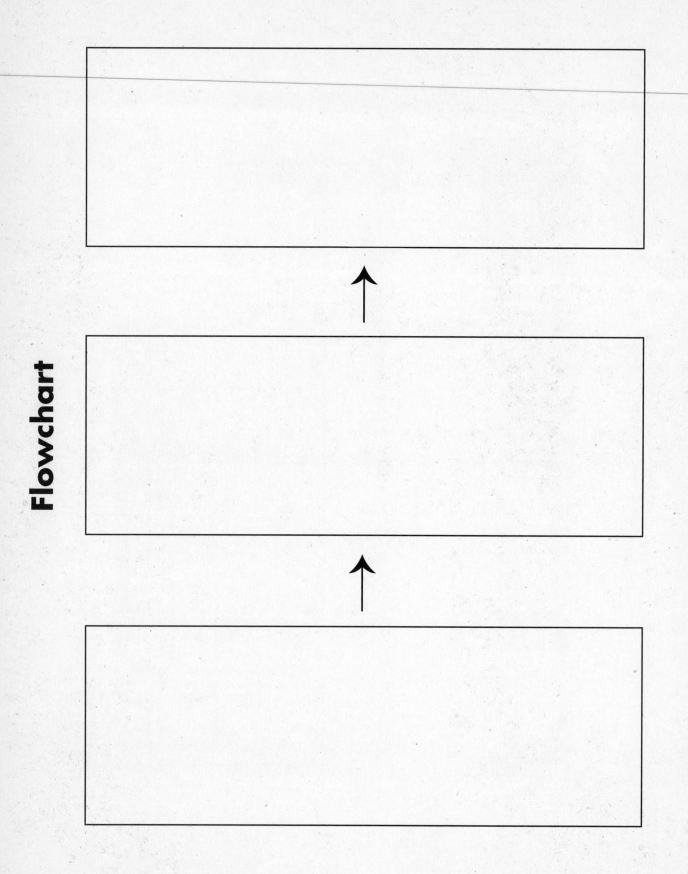

Harcourt

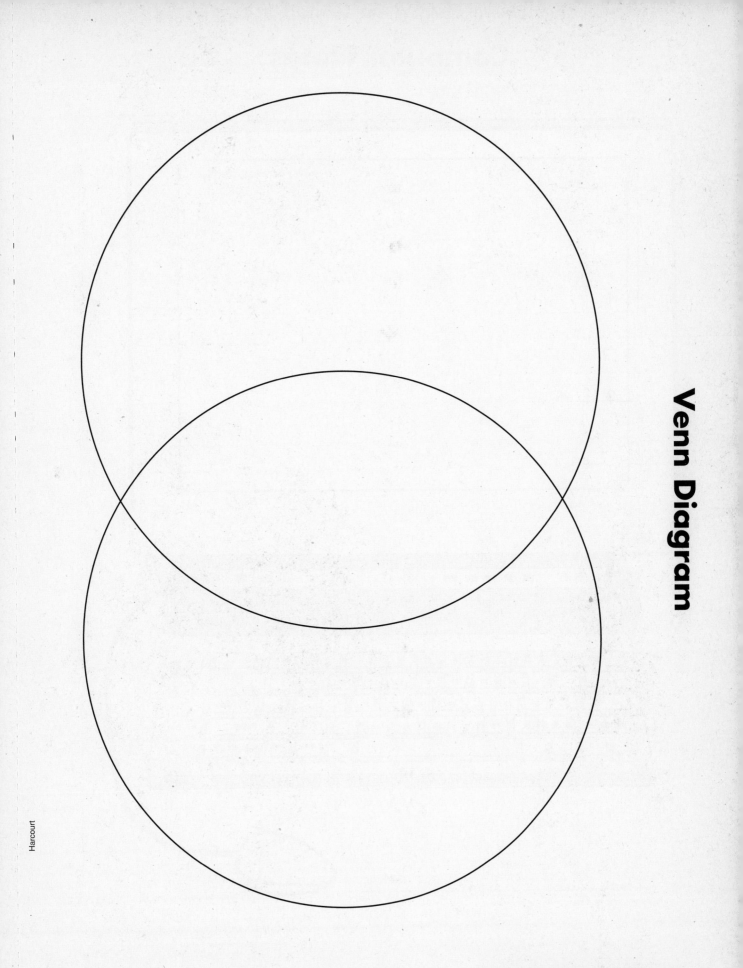

Venn Diagram

Computer Notes

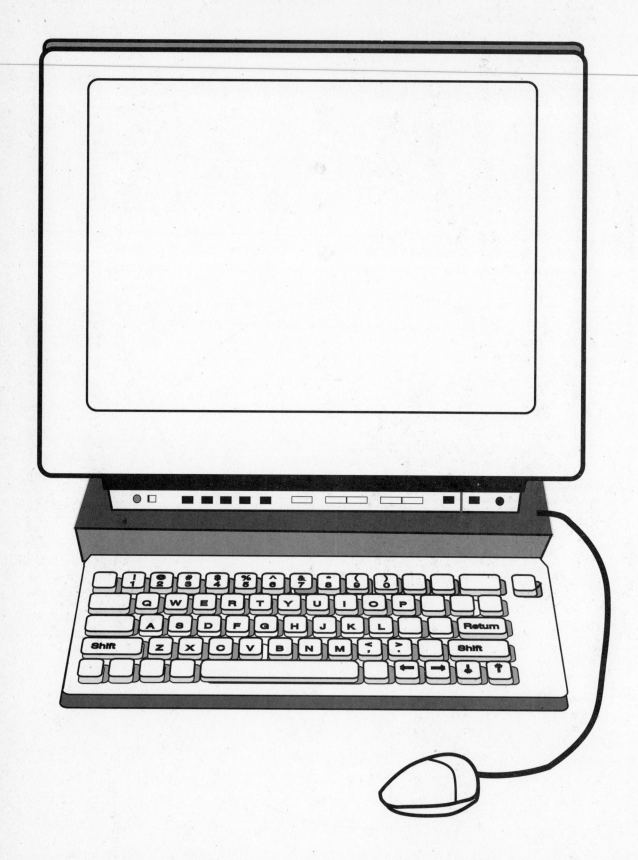

Harcourt

K-W-L Chart

What I Know	What I Want to Know	What I Learned

Harcourt

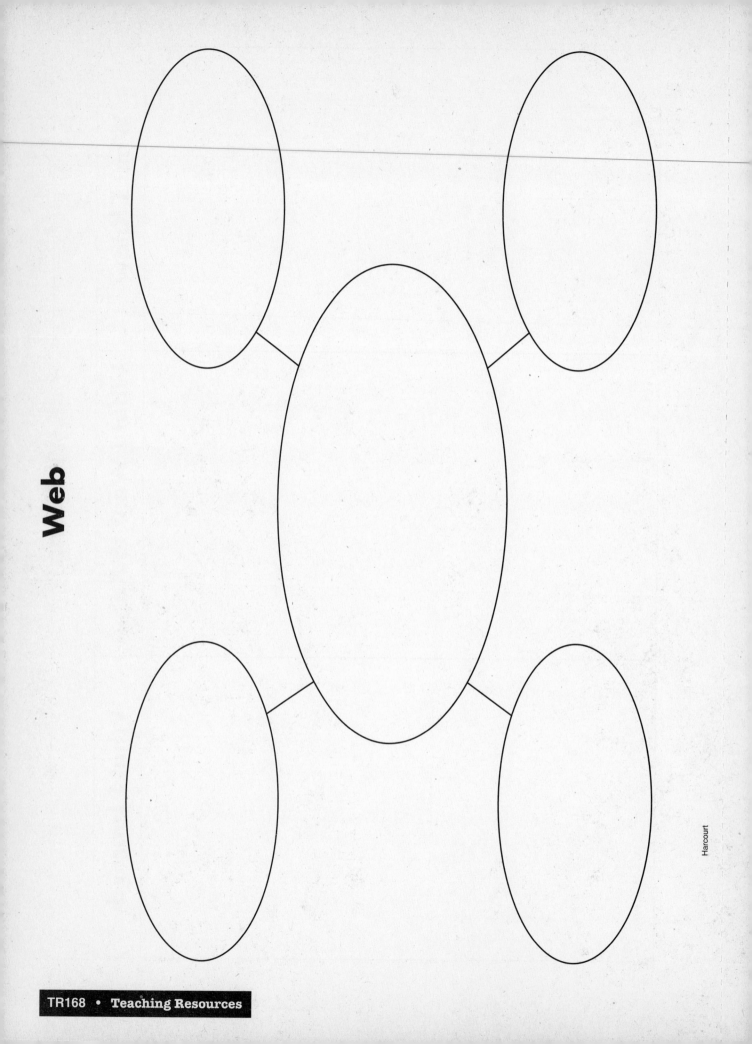

Web

Harcourt

Chart

Knowledge Chart

Prior Knowledge About____	New Knowledge About____
1.	1.
2.	2.
3.	3.
4.	4.
5.	5.
6.	6.
7.	7.

Harcourt

Prediction Chart

What I Predict Will Happen	What Actually Happened

Project Plan

What We Want to Find Out

1.

How We Can Find Out

2.

What We Need to Do

3.   Materials

How We Can Share Information

4.

Harcourt

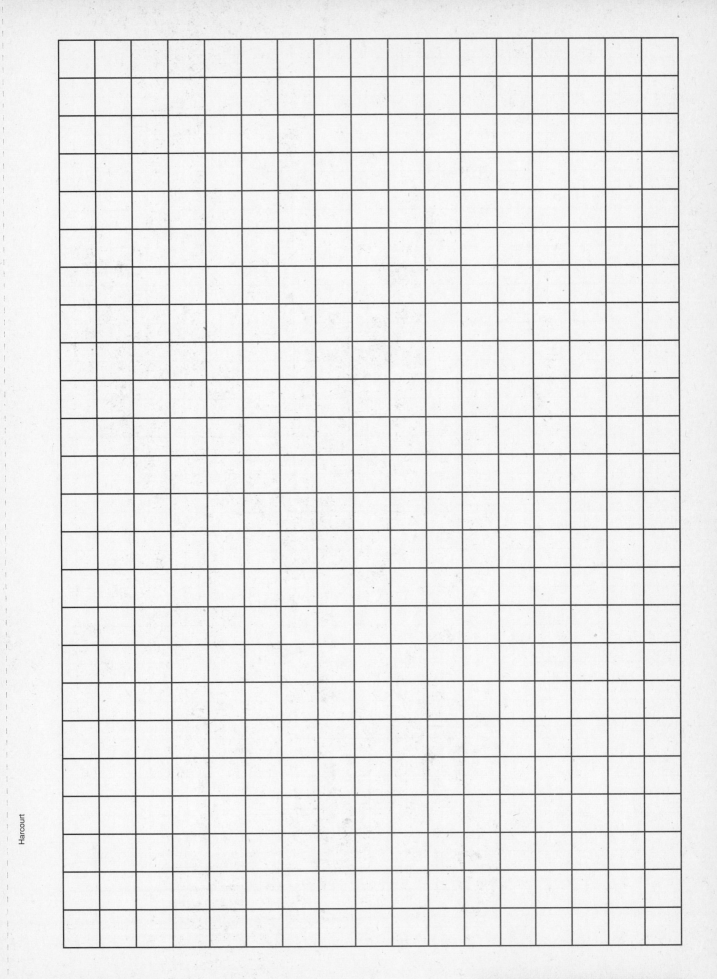

Harcourt

1-cm grid

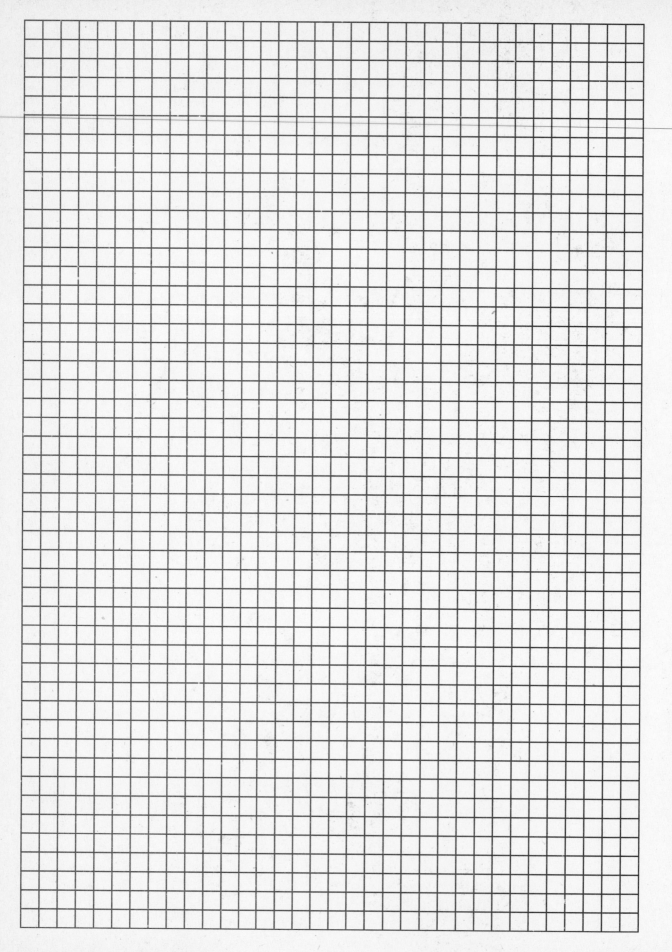

0.5-cm grid